ILLUSTRATED SOURCES IN HISTORY

POVERTY IN ENGLAND 1601-1936

ILLUSTRATED SOURCES IN HISTORY

POVERTY
IN ENGLAND
1601-1936

N. J. SMITH

DAVID & CHARLES : Newton Abbot

BARNES & NOBLE BOOKS : New York
(a division of Harper & Row Publishers, Inc.)

This edition first published in 1972 ✓
in Great Britain by
David & Charles (Publishers) Limited
Newton Abbot   Devon
in the U.S.A. by
Harper & Row Publishers, Inc.
Barnes & Noble Import Division
0 7153 5677 1 *(Great Britain)*
~~06 4963721~~ *(United States)*
© N. J. SMITH, 1972

Set in 10 on 12pt Plantin
by C. E. Dawkins (Typesetters) Limited
London SE1
and printed in Great Britain

CONTENTS

INTRODUCTION

In 1601 the Elizabethan Poor Law acknowledged that there was so much distress in England that governmental steps were necessary to deal with it. Over three hundred years later, in 1936, the government was concerning itself with 'special areas', where the collapse of traditional industries had thrown a large proportion of the population out of work. The problems were different but the product, poverty, was unchanged. The centuries in between had witnessed countless attempts to recognise, and cancel out, the many factors which gave rise to poverty or perpetuated it; but as society grew more complex, and the economic structure of the country shifted and changed, so the aspects of poverty multiplied and took new forms, defeating attempts to forecast, and nullify, their causes.

General patterns did emerge, but even then recognition was not the prelude to cure. The two main trends affecting the condition of the people during these centuries were the great increase in population and the failure of wages to adjust to prices, but their ramifications were so widespread that it proved impossible to control their effect. The course of these trends could be charted and plotted, and predictions could be made, but nothing short of a radical upheaval in society could resolve the problems created.

After 150 years of slow growth, the second half of the eighteenth century saw a spectacular rise in population which has continued, or accelerated, ever since (apart from a short period after World War I). Many theories have been put forward to explain this increase, but all that need concern us is that it took place. The population of England and Wales was an estimated $5\frac{1}{4}$ million in 1600, and about 7 million in 1750—a slow rate of increase. Thereafter, census figures show 8,873,000 in 1801, 17,930,000 in 1851, 36,070,000 in 1911, and 39,952,000 in 1931. There was a shift of population as well as an overall increase, and particular towns grew very fast at various stages—

in the 1820s Manchester's population increased by 47 per cent, in the 1830s Birmingham's went up by 40 per cent, and between 1801 and 1851 London's rose from 1,117,000 to 2,685,000.

Such sudden increases could not be absorbed satisfactorily into existing society. There was a need for more jobs, greater production, more accommodation, and more food; and it was impossible for all these needs to be met in their entirety in a way which did not conflict with vested interests. Where a conflict did exist, the requirements of capital took precedence. There was an increased demand for labour in towns after the Industrial Revolution, but the availability of jobs did not keep pace with the rapid growth of the labour supply, and the work afforded by the factory system was not of the sort calculated to improve a poor man's condition in life. The agricultural worker was also a victim of the increase in population, despite the need for more food. Where there was improved yield, it was at the expense of the old methods of farming, and the labourer lost his patch of land. Later, when demand was such that England had to rely heavily on imported food, farmers found that foreign competition pushed their prices down considerably. Both these trends resulted in rural depopulation, and many agricultural workers turned to the cities for their livelihood, only to join the growing ranks of the urban poor. During the hundred years from 1760 to 1860 the construction of canals and then railways brought some relief to the countryside—gangs of navvies (a thousand strong during the railway-building era) attracted new hands from every village on their route—but this relief was distinctly regional in character. Moreover the navvies lived a brawling, dangerous, nomadic existence, and did not bring any stability to the areas through which they passed.

Emigration was early seen as an answer to over-population, and in the seventeenth century we hear of a plan to 'transport divers idle young people' to Virginia, where they might be set to work. In the nineteenth century the government sponsored emigration committees, the Emigrant Aid Society was founded, and Joseph Arch, the founder of a union for agricultural workers, negotiated an emigration scheme with the Canadian government. Despite all these steps, however, it would be wrong to lay too much stress on the importance of emigration in the fight against poverty. Cobbett, attacking the emigration committees in 1825, emphasised that the poor were rooted in their environment and would be incapable of surviving if thrown on their resources in a strange, uncultivated land. The poor themselves seemed to subscribe to this view, and though 0.84 per cent of the population of Britain emigrated in 1850 (to the USA, Canada, and Australia) many of these were Irish, driven out by the years of famine, and the English emigrants were often men used to regular work who had suddenly fallen on hard times—their self-reliance had not been blunted by years of poverty. For the poor, in fact, migration appeared as a two-edged weapon, for there was a steady movement of cheap Irish labour into England from the eighteenth century onwards.

The other factor to have a general application, the failure of wages to adjust to rising prices, involves the assessment of the real value of money. This, in one age as compared to another, is always hard to establish, but where the poor are concerned the task is made simpler because only the cost of basic necessities is relevant. Here we have to look for regional, and occupational, variation. In some areas the price of fuel was significant—in eighteenth-century Exeter, for instance, fuel cost the poorer classes about one-seventh of their income—but in other areas, such as coal-mining districts, or agricultural districts where common land still survived, fuel was either very cheap or gathered free. The same disparity is found in the payment of rent. This item accounted for one-eighth of a Rotherham foundry-man's wage in 1770, and one-fifth of the wage of the average Northampton working man in 1923; but farm labourers with tied cottages usually had no rent to pay at all.

Thus such outgoings as rent and payment for fuel had different priorities in different parts of the country; but food, of course, was at the top of the list wherever a person lived. As bread was the staple diet throughout most of the period (to be displaced by potatoes, and to a lesser extent meat, in the twentieth century), the cost of corn was for a long time the all-important consideration. A bad harvest meant that prices would be very high, and a glut brought a uniform fall, but such happenings were sporadic, and rarely allowed for; the wage-earner simply had to suffer or benefit as the market dictated. Between these two extremes were trends in prices which were more consistent, and it is these that we must use as a guide to the relative value of money. Farmers and manufacturers, however, employed no such guide; they were concerned with increasing their profits, and recognised no social obligation to adjust wages according to the cost of living.

The imbalance between wages and food prices is best illustrated by specific examples. It is easy, for instance, to plot the fortunes of farm labourers around Exeter in the period from 1740 to 1790—in that time wages remained static at 8s a week, but corn rose from 28s 8d a quarter in 1759 to 55s 6d a quarter in 1791. A more drastic example is that of the stocking-makers of Leicester in 1816. They had to accept a 40 per cent cut in wages in a year when corn at one time reached 165s a quarter. Fifty years later corn was selling at an average of 52s a quarter, whilst wages in most manufacturing towns were a comfortable 15s a week or more, clear evidence that prosperity was being enjoyed by most classes in society. Yet when foreign corn pushed the price down to 27s at the end of the century—less than it had been 150 years before—the evidence pointed in a different direction. This price has to be seen in the context of a general slump in prices, which caused wage reductions and unemployment. Moving into the twentieth century, we find that the cost of food rose 236 per cent between 1914 and 1919 (the war years) but wages failed to keep up; and in 1930, one of the years of depression, the average wage throughout the country was only 33s 6d although a man with a wife and three children needed a minimum of 35s a week.

Thus the picture emerges of a section of society continually subjected to the harmful consequences of social and economic change. The extracts which make up this book add detail to the picture, on the one hand illustrating the various characteristics of poverty, and the behaviour and attitudes that sprang from it, and on the other hand outlining or assessing the remedies which were attempted. As the whole problem covered such a wide field, anyone who came into contact with it had a relevant comment to make (even works showing obvious bigotry or misunderstanding have their importance, for climates of opinion influenced attempts to reach a solution). For this reason the sources include novelists and poets as well as biographers, economists, and historians. The achievements that have been recorded over these three hundred years were not great, but at least the complexities of poverty were gradually recognised, and more understanding developed of its deleterious effect—few people today think that vices create poverty instead of the other way round. Sadly, progress towards greater understanding has been punctuated from time to time by measures which gave priority to administrative efficiency at the expense of charitable intention.

The first chapter traces a number of trends which threatened the interests of groups slow to adjust to them. As new economic conditions developed, so difficulties were encountered throughout society, but it was the poor who bore the main brunt of the hardships and increased costs involved, in the short term at least. A point to remember here is that these trends were usually regional in character; a period of depression in Liverpool could coincide with a period of relative prosperity in Leeds, and the plight of the Wiltshire farm labourer in the nineteenth century gives us no clue to the condition of his counterpart in Lancashire.

Chapters Two and Three are concerned with the poor man's attempts to gain relief from his condition in life. Religion provided comfort for some. There was satisfaction to be gained from leading a life of virtue, rising above the surrounding squalor and vice; and the suffering of the poor, as long as it was stoically borne, was regarded as an added qualification for salvation. In a more transient way, games and pastimes could play their part in providing relief and contentment. But, as will be seen, many of these were brutal and degrading, reflecting the destructive influences at work on the standards of the poor, and on the whole it seems that innocent, healthy enjoyment was rarely present. When a man used what leisure he had simply to blot out the memory of his daily life, there was little chance that he could improve his condition and achieve any real sense of satisfaction. Leisure activities which complemented labour were a great rarity among the poor, despite romantic notions to the contrary.

Relief of another sort was the aim of the corporate attempts to win concessions from governments or employers. In this field we find that the efforts of the poorer classes progressed from crude violence to constructive proposals and demands supported by the threat of concerted action. Mob rule made the forces of law and order fearful of the 'inflammable populace', and the authorities turned to repressive and brutal action in retaliation. The more sophisticated protests of later working-class movements met with the same reaction from time to time, especially as peaceful intentions were sometimes overridden in the heat of the moment, turning orderly demonstra-tions into riots. Employers encouraged, and lobbied for, firm action by the agencies of government, as well as developing their own means of thwarting the workers' ends, so that the whole history of the reaction against poverty has been accompanied by an atmos-phere of suspicion and hostility. The trade unions of the twentieth century, wide though their influence is, have never overcome this handicap. Their legal rights have been extended and their organisation has improved, but lack of co-operation between them and their employers has frequently made bargaining difficult.

The last three chapters illustrate stages in the fight against poverty from the outside. The first stage was that in which people endowed with a generous share of compassion observed the state of the poor and saw where they could take action to bring about an improvement. Sometimes this action consisted of setting up institutions with specific functions—hospitals, and homes or schools for children provide the most obvious examples. Other philanthropists initiated campaigns or societies to provide services on a more general scale, or to inspire governments to accept responsibility for fighting the consequences of poverty. Ultimately the work of these individuals and groups brought about a national awareness, which in turn led to a sense of public responsibility.

From this point we move on to a consideration of the efforts of the legislators, though it should not be assumed that enacted measures to help the poor were always effective in practice. There has always been opposition to poor relief. Undeserving cases have inevitably taken advantage of particular provisions and this fact has strengthened widely held beliefs that the poor should fend for themselves. Self-righteous payers of taxes and poor rates did their best to block poor law legislation which would increase their financial burden, and where a Bill could not be defeated its provisions were often circumvented by local authorities, particularly in the eighteenth century. Employers, on their part, often felt that laws regulating conditions of service were directly against their interests, and an examination of the activities of the guilds of the seventeenth century, or the factory owners of the nineteenth century, will show that abuses continued long after laws were passed to remove them.

Initially the aim of the legislators went no further than to save the poor from destitution, but as a result of the pressure and example of the philanthropists, government extended its role and tried to protect the poor from the forces which created misery. Later still, measures were introduced to raise people out of poverty; from the late nineteenth century onwards a number of laws were passed with the objective of undermining conditions and behaviour patterns which caused poverty to flourish. In this sphere much of the work was directed towards freeing children from the consequences of their background by providing education, free meals, and free medical attention (though as child welfare was the particular concern of so many philanthropists I have preferred to select sources in this field dealing with their work, rather than with that of the legislators).

In the last chapter I have examined steps taken for the relief of the destitute poor. For a long time the purpose of these measures was mainly to protect society from exploitation by the lazy, and the laws that were passed generally aimed to make life hard for the man who would not work; it was not until the twentieth century that real progress was made in the attempts to link aid for the destitute poor with the constructive measures being adopted to help the labouring poor.

Finally an extract from the 1937 Report on the British Social Services has been selected, which points out the limitations of the social reforms carried out up to that date, and of the thinking behind them.

CHAPTER ONE

THE VICTIMS OF ECONOMIC TRENDS

Increases in population, price fluctuations, variable markets and new methods of production produced economic upheavals in which the chief sufferers were the labouring classes. Employers and landowners had their own interests to serve first when dealing with new economic circumstances, and in protecting these they could always claim that they were serving the long-term interests of their employees and dependents—if the master recovered his prosperity, he could afford to look after his workmen. Those of tender conscience, moreover, would often point to factors creating poverty which could not be laid to their charge, such as bad harvests, poor housing, or overpopulation.

Enclosure

Sheep farming proved very profitable in the sixteenth and seventeenth centuries, so many landowners fenced off their holdings for this purpose, taking over common land as well in most cases. These enclosers, and landlords who turned to large-scale farming at the expense of their tenants, were responsible for much suffering. The following extract from 'A PETITION TO PARLIAMENT AGAINST ENCLOSURE OF LAND*' (1649) describes the harmful consequences of enclosure in a part of Leicestershire.*

. . . your petitioners with much confidence, present to your Consideracion one great occasion of the Increase and cry of the poore amonge us, and an impediment to common commerce and traffique which arise from many discords and Abuses both in Intercommoning and Inclosinge of Common feilds amonge us. By Inclosinge (which is now very frequent) there being within these two yeare within these two Counties at least [blank] townes taken in and Inclosed and many other Townes agitateing thereof. Tillage doth daylie decay whereby many of the inhabitants are constrayned either for want of worke, or through cruelty of Landlords to fly to other places and especially to markett townes, whereby they are not onely opprest with multitude of poore, but disabell

to mainetaine them through the Decay of the markett, and traffique; unto which there is further obstruction of mutuall traffique added by this Inclosure of Common feilds: that the highwayes become impassable for travellers.

In THE CASE OF THE LABOURER IN HUSBANDRY (1795), *the Rev David Davies was very concerned by the way in which small-holders were losing their lands to engrossers. Apart from the effect of this trend on the rural economy, he saw it as undermining the people's sense of social responsibility.*

1st. The *land-owner*, to render his income adequate to the increased expence of living, unites several small farms into one, raises the rent to the utmost, and avoids the expence of repairs. The rich farmer also engrosses as many farms as he is able to stock;

1 *Haymaking in the early seventeenth century (from the* Roxburgh Ballads). *Men earned an average of 8d a day, women half that*

lives in more credit and comfort than he could otherwise do; and out of the profits of several farms, makes an ample provision for one family. Thus thousands of families, which formerly gained an independent livelihood on those separate farms, have been gradually reduced to the class of day-labourers. But day-labourers are sometimes in want of work, and are sometimes unable to work; and in either case their sole resource is the parish. It is a fact, that thousands of parishes have not now half the number of farmers which they had formerly. And in proportion as the number of farming families has decreased, the number of poor families has increased.

13

2ndly. The depriving the peasantry of all landed property has beggared multitudes. It is plainly agreeable to sound policy, that as many individuals as possible in a state should possess an interest in the soil; because this attaches them strongly to the country and its constitution, and makes them zealous and resolute in defending them. But the gentry of this kingdom seem to have lost sight of this wise and salutary policy. Instead of giving to labouring people a valuable stake in the soil, the opposite measure has so long prevailed, that but few cottages, comparatively, have now *any* land about them. Formerly many of the lower sort of people occupied tenements of their own, with parcels of land about them, or they rented such of others. On these they raised a considerable part of their subsistence, without being obliged, as now, to buy all they want at shops. And this kept numbers from coming to the parish. But since those small parcels of ground have been swallowed up in the contiguous farms and inclosures, and the cottages themselves have been pulled down; the families which used to occupy them are crowded together in decayed farm-houses, with hardly ground enough about them for a cabbage garden: and being thus reduced to be mere hirelings, they are of course very liable to come to want.

Benjamin Disraeli, who was later Prime Minister, chose the medium of the novel for his social comment on the England of 1845. The following extract from SYBIL *or* THE TWO NATIONS *shows that even in his time depopulation of agricultural areas was producing the worst symptoms of poverty in the smaller towns.*

. . . Marney mainly consisted of a variety of narrow and crowded lanes formed by cottages built of rubble, or unhewn stones without cement, and, from age or badness of the material, looking as if they could scarce hold together. The gaping chinks admitted every blast; the leaning chimneys had lost half their original height; the rotten rafters were evidently misplaced; while in many instances the thatch,

2 *Disraeli*

yawning in part to admit the wind and the wet, and in all utterly unfit for its original purpose of giving protection from the weather, looked more like the top of a dunghill than a cottage. Before the doors of these dwellings, and often surrounding them, ran open drains full of animal and vegetable refuse, decomposing into disease, or sometimes in their imperfect course filling foul pits or spreading into stagnant pools . . .

These wretched tenements seldom consisted of more than two rooms, in one of which the whole family, however numerous, were obliged to sleep, without distinction of age, or sex, or suffering. With the water streaming down the walls, the light distinguished through the roof, with no hearth even

14

in winter, the virtuous mother in the sacred pangs of childbirth gives forth another victim to our thoughtless civilisation; surrounded by three generations whose inevitable presence is more painful than her sufferings in that hour of travail; while the father of her loving child, in another corner of the sordid chamber, lies stricken by that typhus which his contaminated dwelling has breathed into his veins, and for whose next prey is perhaps destined his new-born child . . .

This town of Marney was a metropolis of agricultural labour, for the proprietors of the neighbourhood having for the last half-century acted on the system of destroying the cottages on their estates, in order to become exempted from the maintenance of the population, the expelled people had flocked to Marney, where, during the war, a manufactory had afforded them some relief, though its wheels had long ceased to disturb the waters of the Mar.

Guilds

Masters of particular crafts and trades had formed themselves into guilds, which survived well into the eighteenth century in one form or another. These guilds ensured that their interests were protected from employees and rivals alike, as is illustrated by the FELTMAKERS' COURT BOOK *of 1698.*
We whose hands are hereunto subscribed and sett being Journeymen Feltmakers in and about the City of London and Borough of Southwark doe hereby acknowledge: That we with other Journeymen of the said Trade have held severall meetings wherein we have conspired and combined together to enhance the prices for making of Hats for which severall of us now stand indicted. And being now greatly sensible and fully convinced of the unlawfulness of such conspiracies, Doe hereby declare our hearty and unfeigned sorrow for the same, and we and every-one of us doe hereby promise and agree to and with the Master, Wardens and Commonalty of the Company of Feltmakers London, that neither we nor any of us (nor any other journeyman of the Trade with out or any of our privity and consent) shall or will at any time hereafter doe any act or thing whatsoever that may in any wise tend to the promoting or encouraging of such conspiracies or combinations . . .

In the case of the Norwich weavers, their guild appealed successfully to Parliament. Daniel Defoe, writing anonymously, recorded their victory over calico weavers in A TOUR THRO' THE WHOLE ISLAND OF GREAT BRITAIN (1724). *Defoe, generally unsympathetic towards the poor (as were many people in his time), liked to emphasise examples of industrious prosperity.*
An Eminent Weaver of *Norwich*, gave me a Scheme of their Trade on this Occasion, by which, calculating from the number of Looms at that time employed in the City of *Norwich* only, besides those employ'd in other Towns in the same County, he made it appear very plain, that there were 120,000 People employ'd in the Woollen and Silk and Wool Manufactures of that City only; not that the People all lived in the City, tho' *Norwich* is a very large and populous City too: But I say, they were employ'd for spinning the Yarn used for such Goods as were all made in that City. This Account is Curious enough, and very exact, but it is too long for the compass of this Work.

This shows the Wonderful Extent of the *Norwich* Manufacture, or Stuff weaving Trade, by which so many thousands of Families are maintained. Their Trade indeed felt a very sensible Decay, and the Cries of the Poor began to be very loud, when the weaving of painted Callicoes was grown to such an *height* in *England*, as was seen about two or three Years ago; but an Act of Parliament having been obtain'd, tho' not without great Struggle, in the Years 1720, and 1721, for prohibiting the use and wearing of Callico's, the Stuff Trade reviv'd incredibly; and as I pass'd this part of the Country in the Year 1723, the Manufacturers assured me, that there was not in all the Eastern and Middle part of *Norfolk*,

16

any Hand, unemploy'd, if they would Work; and that the very Children after four or five Years of Age, could everyone earn their own Bread.

In his classic work on political economy, THE WEALTH OF NATIONS (1776), *Adam Smith exposed the collusion among employers to control wages.*

Masters are always and everywhere in a sort of tacit, but constant and uniform, combination, not to raise wages of labour above their actual rate. To violate this combination is everywhere a most unpopular action, and a sort of reproach to a master among his neighbours and equals. We seldom hear of this combination because it is the usual, and, one may say, the natural state of things . . . Masters too sometimes enter into particular combinations to sink the wages of labour even below this rate. These are always conducted with the utmost silence and secrecy . . .

Wages and Prices

The failure of wages to keep pace with prices was one of the most regular causes of poverty from the eighteenth century onwards. IN THE CASE OF THE LABOURER IN HUSBANDRY (1795) *the Rev Davies produced a detailed family budget, which, besides showing the disparity between income and expenditure, provided information concerning the diet of the poor.*

Easter 1787 Barkham, Berks.
Weekly expences of a Family, consisting of a Man and his Wife, and five Children, the eldest eight years of age, the youngest an Infant.

	s	d
FLOUR: 7½ gallons, at 10d. per *gallon* ..	6	3
Yeast, to make it into bread, 2½d; and salt ..	0	4
Bacon, 1 lb. boiled at two or three times with greens: the pot-liquor, with bread and potatoes, makes a mess for the Children ..	0	8

3 *Cottage industry in the late eighteenth century.*
A drawing by J. C. Ibbotson

Tea, 1 ounce, 2d; ¾lb. sugar, 6d; ½lb. butter or lard 4d	1	0
Soap, ¼lb. at 9d *per* lb.	0	2¼
Candles, ⅓lb. one week with another at a medium, at 9d	0	3
Thread, thrum, and worsted, for mending apparel, &c.	0	3

Total 8 11¼

[*Annual outgoings (rent, fuel, clothing, midwife, etc) were assessed at £7. Average weekly earnings of the man and his wife were 8s 6d.*]

Feb 1789 (communicated through Thomas Stanley, Esq; M.P.)

Man, wife, 5 children, 11 down, from Preston.

Expences per Week	£	s	d
Bread from Oatmeal	0	3	0
Potatoes	0	0	9
Salt	0	0	3
Bacon or other meat	0	0	4
Tea, Sugar, Treacle, Butter	0	0	11½
Beer and Milk	0	0	5
Soap, Starch, and Blue	0	0	4
Candles	0	0	3½
Thread, Thrum, Worsted	0	0	2

Total 0 6 6

[*Annual expenses were assessed at £10 7s 0d. The man's average earnings were 6s 6d a week, the woman's 1s, the children's 2s. Altogether, the family's deficit was £2 11s 0d a year.*]

The Machine Age

The Machine Age created many evils for the populations of the new towns (see Chapter 5), but its adverse economic effects were felt most drastically in areas which had been noted for their cottage industry. The radical reformer William Cobbett produced RURAL

18

RIDES (1830) *to expose the callousness and indifference which created distress in the countryside. Below are his observations on the decay of the Wiltshire cloth trade.*

The villages down this Valley of Avon, and, indeed, it was the same in almost every part of this country, and in the north and west of Hampshire also, used to have great employment for the women and children in the carding and spinning of wool for the making of broadcloth. This was a very general employment for the women and girls; but it is now wholly gone; and this has made a great change in the condition of the people, and in the state of property and of

4 *William Cobbett (1762-1835), a tireless campaigner for social reform and for the extension of the right to vote*

5 *Three machines made obsolete by the Industrial Revolution. The wheel wound the thread on to the spindles; the frame produced a warp; and the loom on the left wove the cloth*

manners and of morals . . .

. . . Now, if by using a machine we can get our coat with less labour than we got it before, the machine is a desirable thing. But, then, mind, we must have the machine at home, and we ourselves must have the profit of it; for if the machine be elsewhere; if it be worked by other hands; if other persons have the profit of it; and if, in consequence of the existence of the machine, we have hands at home who have nothing to do, and whom we must keep, then the machine is an injury to us . . .

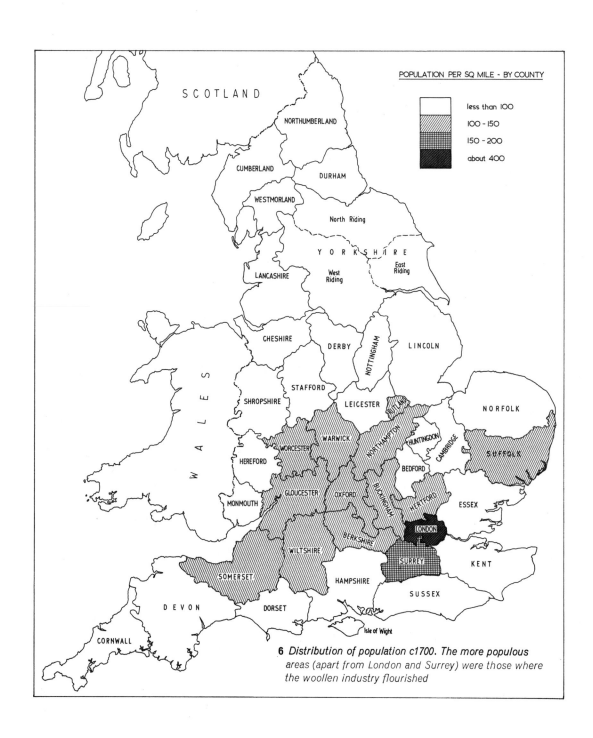

POPULATION PER SQ MILE - BY COUNTY

less than 100
100 - 150
150 - 200
about 400

SCOTLAND

NORTHUMBERLAND

CUMBERLAND

DURHAM

WESTMORLAND

North Riding

Y O R K S H I R E

LANCASHIRE

West Riding

East Riding

CHESHIRE

DERBY

NOTTINGHAM

LINCOLN

STAFFORD

LEICESTER

RUTLAND

NORFOLK

SHROPSHIRE

W A L E S

WORCESTER

WARWICK

NORTHAMPTON

HUNTINGDON

CAMBRIDGE

SUFFOLK

HEREFORD

BEDFORD

GLOUCESTER

OXFORD

BUCKINGHAM

HERTFORD

ESSEX

MONMOUTH

LONDON

BERKSHIRE

WILTSHIRE

SURREY

KENT

SOMERSET

HAMPSHIRE

SUSSEX

DEVON

DORSET

Isle of Wight

CORNWALL

6 *Distribution of population c1700. The more populous areas (apart from London and Surrey) were those where the woollen industry flourished*

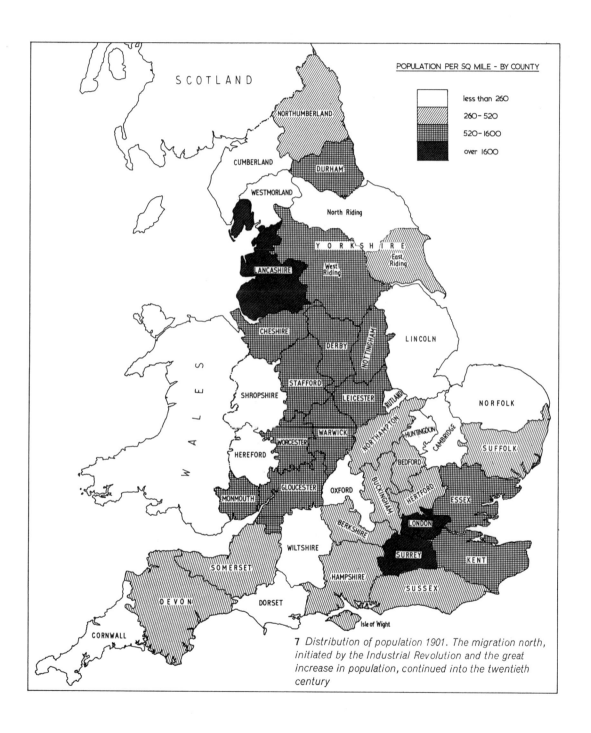

POPULATION PER SQ MILE - BY COUNTY

less than 260
260 - 520
520 - 1600
over 1600

SCOTLAND

NORTHUMBERLAND

CUMBERLAND

DURHAM

WESTMORLAND

North Riding

YORKSHIRE

East Riding

West Riding

LANCASHIRE

CHESHIRE

DERBY

NOTTINGHAM

LINCOLN

W A L E S

SHROPSHIRE

STAFFORD

LEICESTER

RUTLAND

NORFOLK

NORTHAMPTON

HUNTINGDON

CAMBRIDGE

SUFFOLK

WORCESTER

WARWICK

HEREFORD

BEDFORD

MONMOUTH

GLOUCESTER

OXFORD

BUCKINGHAM

HERTFORD

ESSEX

LONDON

BERKSHIRE

SURREY

KENT

WILTSHIRE

SOMERSET

HAMPSHIRE

SUSSEX

DEVON

DORSET

Isle of Wight

CORNWALL

7 *Distribution of population 1901. The migration north, initiated by the Industrial Revolution and the great increase in population, continued into the twentieth century*

James Caird, in ENGLISH AGRICULTURE 1850-1851 (1852) *noted the struggle for existence of the Derbyshire stocking-knitters.*

In Bakewell there are no poor but the frame-stocking knitters, who were established in their trade before power-looms were invented. They still continue to work at a business to which they were brought up, although it scarcely now affords them maintenance.

Not all rural areas suffered from the Industrial Revolution. The following extract from James Caird shows the benefit it brought to farming communities in the North.

The disparity of wages paid for the same nominal amount of work in the various counties of England, is so great as to show that there must be something in the present state of the law affecting the labourer, which prevents the wages of agricultural labour finding a more natural level throughout the country. Taking the highest rate we have met with—15s. a week in parts of Lancashire, and comparing it with the lowest—6s. a week in South Wilts, and considering the facilities of communication in the present day, it is surprising that so great a difference should continue . . . The influence of manufacturing enterprise is thus seen to add 37 per cent. to the wages of the agricultural labourers of the Northern counties, as compared with those of the South. The line is distinctly drawn at the point where coal ceases to be found, to the south of which there is only one of the counties we visited in which the wages reach 10s. a week, Sussex. The local circumstances of that county explain the cause of labour being there better remunerated; the wealthy population of Brighton, and other places on the Sussex coast, affording an increased market for labour beyond the demands of agriculture.

A comparison with the price of labour in the same counties in 1770 will show this influence clearly. In Cumberland, at that time, the wages of the agricultural labourer were 6s. 6d., in the West Riding 6s., in Lancashire 6s. 6d.; in each of which counties they have since increased fully 100 per cent. In all the Northern counties the increase is about 66 per cent. The increase in the eighteen Southern counties mentioned by Young is under 14 per cent. In some of them there is no increase whatever, the wages of the agricultural labourer in parts of Berkshire and Wilts being precisely the same as they were 80 years ago, and in Suffolk absolutely less. The average wages in 1770 in the Northern counties visited by Young were 6s. 9d.; and of the Southern counties 7s. 6d.

Poverty in the Towns

Charles Booth and B. Seebohm Rowntree made invaluable surveys at the end of the nineteenth century which yielded alarming information about poverty in towns; the conclusions drawn by these social pioneers were alarming too. Below is an extract from Rowntree's POVERTY—A STUDY OF TOWN LIFE (1901).

TABLE SHOWING THE MINIMUM NECESSARY EXPENDITURE PER WEEK FOR FAMILIES OF VARIOUS SIZES

Family	Food		Rent		Household Sundries		Total	
	s	d	s	d	s	d	s	d
1 man	3	0	1	6	2	6	7	0
1 woman	3	0			2	6	7	0
1 man and 1 woman	6	0			3	2	11	8
1 man 1 woman 1 child	8	3	2	6	3	9	14	6
1 man 1 woman 2 children	10	6	4	0	4	4	18	10
1 man 1 woman 3 children	12	9			4	11	21	8

Having established a minimum standard of necessary expenditure, we are now in a position to ascertain what proportion of the population of York are living in 'primary' poverty.

As stated in Chapter II, an estimate was made of

8 *Dudley Street, Seven Dials, by Gustav Doré. A London slum at the end of the nineteenth century*

9 *An early factory in Kent—the hand loom could be fitted into the community pattern*

the earnings of every working-class family in York. In order to ascertain how many of these families were living in a state of 'primary' poverty, the income of each was compared with the foregoing standard, due allowance being made in every case for size of family and rent paid.

Let us now see the result of this examination. No less than 1465 families, comprising 7230 persons,

were living in 'primary' poverty. *This is equal to 15.46 per cent of the wage-earning classes in York, and to 9.91 per cent of the whole population of the city.*

The above estimate, it should be particularly noted, is based upon the assumption that *every penny earned*

10 *A print of 1832 showing the twist factory in Oxford Street, Manchester. Factories like this, built without community planning, were the cause of congested living conditions in the surrounding districts*

by every member of the family went into the family purse, and was judiciously expended upon necessaries.

The proportion of the population living in poverty in York may be regarded as practically the same as in London, especially when we remember that Mr. Booth's information was gathered in 1887-1892, a period of only average trade prosperity, whilst the York figures were collected in 1899, when trade was unusually prosperous . . .

We have been accustomed to look upon poverty in London as exceptional, but when the result of careful investigation shows that the proportion of poverty in London is practically equalled in what may be regarded as a typical provincial town, we are faced by the startling probability that from 25 to 30 per cent of the town populations of the United Kingdom are living in poverty.

[Booth wrote to Rowntree agreeing with his thesis.]

Apart from wages and prices, poverty could be measured in terms of living conditions, particularly in the crowded districts created by industry such as Rowntree found in parts of York.

Labourer, Foundry, Married. Four rooms. Four children. Steady; work regular. Man has bad eyesight, and poor wage accordingly. Family live in the midst of smoke. Rent cheap on account of smoke. Rent 3s.
Charwoman. Two rooms, Son twenty. Casual labourer. Husband in workhouse. Dirt and drink in plenty. This house shares one water-tap with six other houses, and one closet with two others. Rent 2s.
Labourer. Married. Four rooms. Six children. Filthy to extreme. This house shares one closet with another, and one water-tap with five others. Rent 3s 6d.
Widow. Four rooms. Five children. Women chars. Entrance to house very bad; slaughter-house on each side. House in bad condition. Rent 3s.

The Depression and After

The period between the two world wars saw wage-cuts, short time, and unemployment as the workers'

share of the economic crises which culminated in the Depression. A slump in agricultural prices, causing many farmers to convert from arable to grass, created the situation described by R. R. Enfield in his book AGRICULTURAL CRISIS 1920-23 (1924).

Where the hardship and suffering resulting from the agricultural crisis was most severe, not only in this country but elsewhere, was, as is always the case in a trade depression, among the agricultural labourers . . . With the repeal of the Agriculture Act, the Agricultural Wages Board came to an end, and the statutory minimum wages ceased to operate after October, 1921. The labourer, whose high hopes of an improved standard of living had been based on the transient prosperity of 1917-19, saw his hopes blighted, and the immediate passing away of the better conditions which he had expected, not without reason, might be permanent. Once more he was to be forced back towards the conditions of economic bondage from which such efforts had been made to free him.

At one stage during the crisis of 1929-33 there were over three million unemployed in Britain. LOVE ON THE DOLE (1933) *by Walter Greenwood (the first truly proletarian novelist) painfully recorded the shame and despair generated by the Depression.*

An erstwhile reformatory school for erring boys, an ugly, barrack-like building, serves as one of the Two Cities' labour exchanges. Hemmed in on three sides by slums, tenements and doss houses, the remaining side stares at the gas works and a cattle-loading mound . . .

A high wall, inclosing an asphalt yard, ran round the building. On it was scrawled in chalk, and in letters a foot high: 'Unemployed Mass Meeting Today 3 o'clock.' The handiwork of Communists five or six weeks ago.

Harry Hardcastle, white mercerized cotton scarf wrapped loosely about his neck, a tuft of fair hair protruding from the neb of his oily cap, patches on

the knees and backside of his overalls, stood in a long queue of shabby men, hands in pockets, staring fixedly and unseeing at the ground. At street corners, leaning against house walls or squatting on the kerb stones, were more men, clothes stinking of age, waiting until the queue opposite went into the building when they would take their places in forming another. And all through the day, every quarter-hour, would see another crowd of fresh faces coming to sign the unemployed register at their appointed times.

The day was Monday. The Saturday previous, Harry's apprenticeship, together with those of Tom Hare, Bill Simmons, Jack Lindsay, Sam Hardie and the rest of their contemporaries, had come to an end. They now were fully qualified engineers. They also were qualified to draw the dole.

The REPORT OF THE MINISTRY OF LABOUR, 1934,

11 *The Labour Exchange at Snow Hill, Birmingham during the Depression, 1930. It was not only the poor who were forced to join the dole queue*

revealed that certain towns, which were centres of traditional industries such as coal mining and ship-building, took a long time to recover from the effects of the Depression.

Percentage of *Insured* Workers Unemployed in Distressed and Prosperous Towns 1934

Jarrow	67.8	Greater London	8.6
Gateshead	44.2	Birmingham	6.4
Workington	36.3	Coventry	5.1
Maryport	57.0	Oxford	5.1
Abertillery	49.6	Luton	7.7
Merthyr	61.9	High Wycombe	3.3
Greenock	36.3	St Albans	3.9
Motherwell	37.4	Watford	7.0

George Orwell, who later won fame for Animal Farm *and* 1984, *had a much more sophisticated background than Greenwood, but he too could write of poverty and unemployment from first-hand experience. The following is an extract from* THE ROAD TO WIGAN PIER (1937).

To study unemployment and its effects you have got to go to the industrial areas. In the South unemployment exists, but it is scattered and queerly unobtrusive. There are plenty of rural districts where a man out of work is almost unheard-of, and you don't anywhere see the spectacle of whole blocks of cities living on the dole and the P.A.C. It is only when you lodge in streets where nobody has a job, where getting a job seems about as probable as owning an aeroplane and much less probable than winning fifty pounds in the Football Pool, that you begin to grasp the changes that are being worked in our civilisation . . .

William Beveridge, the man whose 1924 report was adopted as the social charter for post-war Britain, had foreseen the danger of industrial stagnation as early as 1909, when he presented a thesis in UNEMPLOYMENT: A PROBLEM OF INDUSTRY *which still held good in 1936.* The statement that the country is not over-populated, and that its industrial system is still capable of absorbing the growing supply of labour, must always be something of the nature of a prophecy. It is impossible to bring statistics more than up to date. Because up to date industry has expanded, the inference is made that it is still expanding and capable of further expansion. Because this expansion in the past has taken place through alternations of good years and bad years, the inference is made of any particular period of depression that it is only a temporary phase and will give way to renewed prosperity. All this, however, is far from inevitable. It is likely enough that industry will at some time lose all or much of its power of growth. It is possible that any particular depression may be not a temporary phase but the beginning of a lasting decline. The negative or optimistic conclusion—that unemployment is not now being caused by general over-population—must therefore, by its very nature, be always open to a doubt. The positive conclusion, that there are other factors which have caused unemployment in the past and are liable to cause it in the present, is not open to any doubt at all. From the beginning to the end of fifty years of unprecedented industrial expansion unemployment has been recorded continuously, and has passed at intervals of seven to ten years from a normal to an acute phase. This, in itself, is enough to show that unemployment depends not so much on the volume of industry as upon the methods of industry, and, while the methods remain unchanged, will continue or recur however the volume grows. A falling demand for labour may come as a symptom of national decay. A rising demand for labour will be no cure for unemployment.

CHAPTER TWO

RELIGION AND RECREATION AMONG THE POOR

RELIGION

The Church of England held little specific appeal for those stricken by poverty—it was seen as the church of the middle class, and the conformity it taught provided scant consolation for those in the lowest station of society. From the middle of the seventeenth century onwards sects and religious societies grew up which aimed at correcting the deficiencies of the established church, and these considered crusades among the poor to be of the first importance. Their recruits from the slums and cellars were inspired by fiery preachers, who offered salvation to those who followed a strict moral code and showed forebearance in the face of life's hardship. The strong lay organisation of these bodies gave the poor a sense of being wanted, as well as providing them with material comforts when they were in desperate need.

The Quakers

The Society of Friends (Quakers) was built up, despite persecution, during the Commonwealth period.

Its founder, George Fox, established a tradition of ministering to the underprivileged which survives today, though by the end of the seventeenth century its converts among the poor were few. FOX'S JOURNAL of 1660 contains numerous references, such as the one below, to the charitable actions which attracted the poor to his meetings.

And Justices & Captaines had come to breake uppe this meetinge & then when they saw freinds bookes & accounts of collections concerneinge ye poore how y^t wee did take care one county to helpe another; & tooke care to helpe freindes beyond ye seas & y^t ye poore neede not trouble there parishes: ye Justices were made to confess y^t wee did there worke (& freinds desired y^m to come & sett with y^m then).

And so they passed away loveingely & commended freinds practise.

And many times there woulde bee two hundred beggars of ye worlde there for all ye country knewe wee mett about ye poore which after ye meetinge

12 *An old print showing a Quaker being persecuted during Cromwell's Protectorate. The caption beneath read:* 'James Nailor Quaker set 2 howers on the Pillory at Westminster whiped by the Hangman to the old Exchainge London, Som dayes after, stood too howers more on the Pillory at the Exchainge, and there had his Tongue Bored through with a hot iron, & Stigmatized in the Forehead with the Letter: B: Decem[r] 17 anno Dom 1656'

was donne freinds woulde sende to ye bakers & give y[m] each a loafe a piece bee y[m] as many as woulde.

The Methodists

John Wesley, the father of Methodism, was responsible for a great religious revival among the poorer classes, which lasted until the middle of the nineteenth century. He taught people to accept their condition, but those who lived by his precepts usually found that they rose above the poverty line. He and his followers were renowned for their eloquence, which brought the poor people flocking to their open-air meetings, and in Wesley's *JOURNAL for May 1742 we find an example of his preaching technique.*

Sund. 30.

At seven I walked down to Sandgate [in New-castle-upon-Tyne], the poorest and most contemptible part of the town, and standing at the end of the street with *John Taylor*, began to sing the hundredth psalm. Three or four people came out to see what was the matter, who soon encreased to four or five hundred. I suppose, there might be twelve or fifteen hundred before I had done preaching: to who I applied those solemn words, *He was wounded for our transgressions, He was bruised for our iniquities; the*

13 *A Quaker meeting. The meetings were addressed by any of the congregation who felt inspired*

chastisement of our peace was upon Him, and by his stripes we are healed.

Observing the people when I had done to stand gaping and staring upon me, with the most profound astonishment, I told them, 'If you desire to know who I am, my name is *John Wesley*. At five in the evening, with God's help, I design to preach here again.'

At five, the hill on which I designed to preach, was cover'd from the top to the bottom. I never saw so large a number of people together . . . The word of God which I set before them was, *I will heal their backsliding, I will love them freely.* After preaching, the poor people were ready to tread me under foot, out of pure love and kindness.

Simple instructions and careful organisation were the basis of Methodism, as will be seen from the following directives Wesley gave to his followers in A PLAIN ACCOUNT OF THE PEOPLE CALLED METHODISTS (1749). *Once a man had joined the society, his class leader worked hard to ensure his continuance in the faith.*

There is One only condition previously required, in those who desire Admission into this Society, *A desire to flee from the Wrath to come, and to be saved from their Sins.* But whevever this Desire is fixt in the Soul, it will be shewn by its Fruits. It is therefore expected of all who continue therein, that they should continue to evidence their Desire of Salvation.

First, By doing no Harm, by avoiding Evil in every kind; especially that which is most generally practised.

(Such as, The taking of the Name of GOD in vain; the profaning the Day of the LORD; Drunkenness; Fighting, Quarrelling, Brawling; the Buying or Selling uncustom'd Goods; The doing to others as we would not they should do unto us; Uncharitable or Unprofitable Conversation, particularly, Speaking evil of Magistrates or Ministers:)

Secondly, By doing Good, by being in every kind merciful after their Power; As they have opportunity, doing Good of every possible Sort, and as far as it is possible to all Men: . . .

It is the Business of a Leader

I. To see each Person in his Class, once a Week at the least;

In order,

To enquire how their Souls prosper?
To advise, reprove, comfort or exhort, as Occasion may require;
To receive what they are willing to give, toward the relief of the Poor.

II. To meet the Minister and the Stewards of the Society, in order
To inform the Minister of any
that are Sick, or of any that are
Disorderly and will not be reproved;
To pay to the Stewards what they have receiv'd of their several Classes in the Week preceding.

The Chapels

Tightly-knit congregations, inspired by the fervour of their ministers, prepared themselves for the 'day of reckoning' in the chapels which flourished in the populous towns of the eighteenth and nineteenth centuries. Here they could find solace despite their unhappy worldly state.

THE JOURNALS OF TWO POOR DISSENTERS (*edited by Guida Swan, 1970*) *show how men could be attracted by companionship and the opportunity to perform good works.*

The Journal of William Thomas Swan, born 1786. . . . My new friends were members of Mr Nicholson's Mulberry Gardens Chapel, Pell Street, at which place I attended sometimes, but chiefly I went to Sion Chapel to which place I was much attached because there I had some of the first and the brightest displays of God's goodness in the forgiveness of sins and of man's redemption.

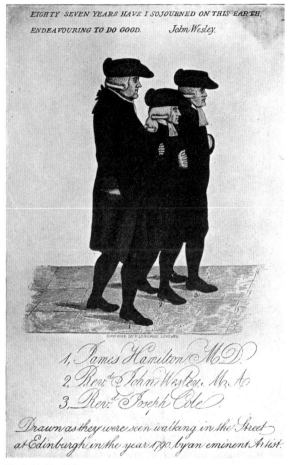

EIGHTY SEVEN YEARS HAVE I SOJOURNED ON THIS EARTH.
ENDEAVOURING TO DO GOOD.   John Wesley.

1, James Hamilton M.D.
2, Revd. John Wesley. M. A.
3, Revd. Joseph Cole.

Drawn as they were seen walking in the Street
at Edinburgh in the year 1790, by an eminent Artist.

14 *A Methodist group*

But Mr Nicholson had been brought up to the church and I needs must hear him. Besides, an old school fellow liv'd near my lodging who was a member, and with him I us'd to have a good Christian conversation, and by him I was introduced to be a teacher in their Sunday school — . . .

[*About 1814 Swan became a Baptist.*]

. . . Some time after joining the church, it so happened that I miss'd an old female, a Mrs Benton, and finding that she was ill I went to see her so repeatedly that it came to Mr Dean, a Deacon's ears. He soon afterwards said to me, 'I'll find you more of this work to do.' Shortly after this, Mr Williams, who was then both Treasurer and Secretary of the Sick Mans Assistant Society, asked me to assist in visiting. This was about the year 1820. At the resignation of Mr W I was called upon to be Secretary for a time but when our numbers were increas'd, a more efficient brother, Mr White, took it on him.

O the felicity to be found in this service! I believe it to be a most important part of religion, to visit the fatherless and widows, the sick and distressed . . .

In SYBIL, *Disraeli recognised class distinction in religion. The poor could find nothing in the Church of England to atone for their condition—they turned instead to the vigorous fervour of the chapels.*

The eyes of this unhappy race might have been raised to the solitary spire that sprang up in the midst of them, the bearer of present consolation, the harbinger of future equality; but Holy Church at Marney had forgotten her sacred mission. We have introduced the reader to the vicar, an orderly man, who deemed he did his duty if he preached each week two sermons, and enforced humility on his congregation, and gratitude for the blessings of this life. The high street and some neighbouring gentry were the staple of his hearers . . . The people of Marney took refuge in conventicles, which abounded; little plain buildings of pale brick, with the names printed on them of Sion, Bethel, Bethesda; names of a distant land, and the language of a persecuted and ancient race; yet such is the mysterious power of their divine quality, breathing consolation in the nineteenth century to the harassed forms and the harrowed souls of a Saxon peasantry.

The Salvation Army

The Salvation Army, led by General Booth, made a dramatic and stirring appeal amidst the misery and decadence of the late nineteenth century. W. T. Stead's

biography of the general's wife—MRS BOOTH OF THE SALVATION ARMY (1900)—*gave evidence of the approach which was so successful in converting the poor.*

My farm-lad Dick used to attend regularly. 'It's as good as a theayter,' he told me. 'You can go in when you like, and if you want a drop or a smoke in the middle, why, out you come, just as you please. But there's some of the biggest blackguards turned convarters now.' By 'convarters' he meant converts; but his word was true, for all The Salvation Army converts are converters . . . At last I went to see the girls who had turned Darlington upside down. I was amazed. I found two delicate girls . . . ministering to a crowded congregation, which they had themselves collected out of the street, and building up an aggressive church militant out of the human refuse which other churches regarded with blank despair. They had come to the town without a friend, without an introduction, with hardly a penny in their purses. They had to provide for maintaining services regularly every week-night, and nearly all day Sunday, in the largest hall in the town . . . these girls raised a new cause out of the ground, in the poorest part of the town, and made it self-supporting by the coppers of their collections. In the first six months, a thousand persons had been down to the penitent-form . . . and a corps or church was formed of nearly 200 members, each of whom was pledged to speak, pray, sing, visit, march in procession, and take a collection.

Revivalism
The high rate of unemployment in the 1920s brought despair to many households, but the religious revivalists fought to spread comfort and hope. Arthur Barton described the Jarrow of his boyhood in TWO LAMPS IN OUR STREET (1967), *and offered reasons for the success (albeit temporary) of the evangelists.*

15 *General Booth*

There seemed to be a great deal of evangelism about in those days. As employment decreased more and more, and men queued for the dole and hung about street corners waiting for better times, one evangelist after another came to our town and played to packed houses. The vacuum left by the departure of a way of life was filled temporarily at any rate by religious emotion. I remember the Marechal, one of General Booth's daughters and 'the best actress in England and nothing to pay' as Uncle Jim said, filling our biggest chapel night after night, and Arnold Bennet . . . and the Cliff College Crusaders, and many others. It was nothing to see weeping girls kneel in the streets, or hear prominent townsmen confessing their instantaneous conversions from a soap box in the market square. But between visits the religious life of the town dropped to its former temperate level. One by one the emotionally converted felt their fervour drain away and languished until the next evangelist whipped it up again.

RECREATION
Until the late nineteenth century cruelty, brutality and strong drink figured prominently in the amusements of the poor; the struggle for survival coarsened the capacity for enjoyment. Later the 56 hour week and) compulsory education—innovations of the 1870s— increased the scope for leisure activity, and the mass entertainments of the twentieth century presented a wider choice. Uninspiring work, however, still left its mark on a man's incentive to develop the range of his interests.

Seventeenth-century Pastimes
Hurling, football, and hand-ball were all variations of the same game. They frequently came under the ban of the magistrates. Richard Carew, in THE SURVEY OF CORNWALL (1602), *showed why.*

The hurling to the countrey, is more diffuse and confuse, as bound to few of these orders: Some two

10 of May the Boocke of Sportes vpon the Lords day was burnt by the Hangman in the place where the Crosse stoode, & at Exhange

16 *During the Puritan Commonwealth, games and pastimes were frowned upon. This engraving by Hollar shows the ceremonial burning of James I's* Book of Sports, *which had authorised certain activities on Sundays*

or more Gentlemen doe commonly make this match, appointing that on such a holyday, they will bring to such an indifferent place, two, three, or more parishes of the East or South quarter, to hurl against so many other of the West or North. Their goales are either those Gentlemens houses, or some townes or villages, three or foure miles asunder, of which either side maketh choice after the neernesse to their dwellings, when they meet, there is neyther comparing of numbers nor matching of men: but a silver ball is cast up, and that company, which can catch, and cary it by force, or sleight, to their place assigned, gaineth the ball and victory. . . .

The Hurlers take their next way ouer hilles, dales, hedges, ditches; yea, and thorow bushes, briers, mires, plashes and riuers whatsoeuer; so as you shall sometimes see 20. or 30. lie tugging together in the water, scrambling and scratching for the ball. A play

(verily) both rude & rough. . . .

I cannot well resolue, whether I should more commend this game, for the manhood and exercise, or condemne it for the boysterousnes and harmes which it begetteth: for as on the one side it makes their bodies strong, hard, and nimble, and puts a courage into their hearts, to meete an enemie in the face: so, on the other part, it is accompanied with many dangers, some of which doe euer fall to the players share. For proofe whereof, when the hurling is ended, you shall see them retyring home as from a pitched battaile, with bloody pates, bones broken, and out of ioynt, and such bruses as serve to shorten their daies; yet al is good play. . . .

Church feasts, May Day and Whit celebrations, and fairs, brought holidays two or three times a year which were eagerly awaited. Below, Carew gives an account of a Whitsun church-ale, and reflects a widespread disapproval of the excesses that attended such functions.

For the Church-ale, two young men of the parish are yerely chosen by their last foregoers, to be Wardens, who deuiding the task, make collection among the parishioners, of whatsoeuer prouision it

17 *Football on Shrove Tuesday at Kingston-on-Thames, 1846. Most of the male population took part*

pleaseth them voluntarily to bestow. This they imploy in brewing, baking, & other acates, against Whitson-tide; vpon which Holydayes, the neighbours meet at the Church-house, and there merily feed on their owne victals, contributing some petty portion to the stock, which by many smalls groweth to a meetly greatnes: for there is entertayned a kinde of emulation between these Wardens, who by his graciousnes in gathering, and good husbandry in expending, can best advance the Churches profit. Besides, the neighbour parishes, at those times louingly visit one another,

and this way frankely spend their money together. . . .

. . . the very title of ale was somewhat nasty, and the thing it selfe had beene corrupted with such a multitude of abuses, to wit, idlenes, drunkennesse, lasciuiousnes, vain disports of ministrelsie, dauncing, and disorderly night-watchings, that the best curing was to cut it cleane away.

Joseph Strutt's SPORTS AND PASTIMES OF THE PEOPLE OF ENGLAND (1801) *was an illustrated history of leisure*

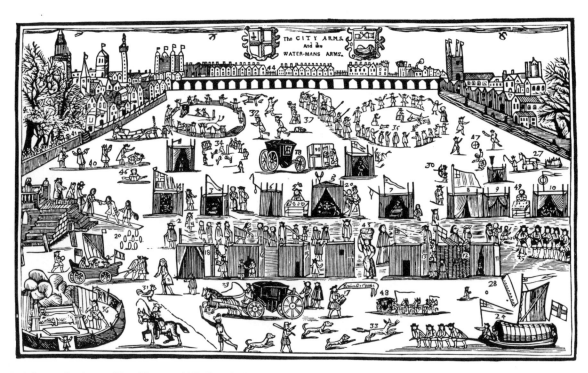

18 *A fair on the frozen River Thames, 1683. Bear-baiting, bull-baiting and skittles are among the activities depicted*

activities, which gave a dispassionate yet full account of the various diversions to be found during the seventeenth and eighteenth centuries.

The Puppet-shows usually made their appearance at great fairs, and especially at those in the vicinity of the metropolis; they still continue to be exhibited in Smithfield at Bartholomewtide, though with very little trace of their former greatness; indeed, of late years, they have become unpopular, and are frequented only by children. It is, however, certain, that the puppet-shows attracted the notice of the public at the commencement of the last century, and rivalled in some degree the more pompous exhibitions of the larger theatres. . . .

In the month of May the citizens of London of all estates, generally in every parish, and in some instances two or three parishes joining together, had their severall mayings, and did fetch their may-poles with divers war-like shews; with good archers, morrice-dancers, and other devices for pastime, all day long; and towards evening they had stage-plays and bonfires in the streets.

Roger Lowe, a Lancashire apprentice, found more time than most of his class to indulge in his pastimes, as his unpublished DIARY (1663-78) *illustrates, but the ale-house was the setting for most of his spare time.*

18 July 1663. I sat forward and upon Latchford Heath there ware a great company of persons with 2 drums amongst them the young men ware playing at prison barrs where I stayd awhile to see them but concluded it was but vanitie. . . .

9 August lords day. Matthew Lythgo Edward
Bradshaw Robert Reynolds came from Leigh sent
for me to Tanks fields and had wenches that mett
them we ware alt aftrnoone in ale house the lord
forgive us. . . .

4 Sept 1663 . . . we went into Watts and spent each
man 2d and made a sett of Bowleing for each man
2d in ale. I was one to bowle and lost. . . .

20 May 1664. John Jenkinson and Joshua Naylor
and I went to gathre to take a throstoll nest and by
chance we met with a py annot nest we tooke every
one had one pye and one we gave to Tho. Winstanly
and so came home. . . .

2 Jan 1665. I went a hunteinge and the hare tooke
into the rabits holes and I was exceedingly wearied. . . .

29 Sept 1667 . . . I went to the castle to see a man
condemned a pretie younge man he was and very sorie
I was. . . .

[*Printed in* LEIGH CHRONICLE, 1877]

*A number of the games in Edward Chamberlayne's
list contained in* ANGLIAE NOTITIA *or* THE PRESENT STATE
OF ENGLAND (1669) *will be unfamiliar. Shovel-board
was a large-scale version of shove-ha'penny; stow-ball
was a variation of tip-cat; goffe was golf; and trol madam
was bagatelle.*

The Citizens and Peasants have *Hand-Ball, Foot-
Ball, Skitles,* or *Nine Pins, Shovel-board, Stow-Ball,
Goffe, Trol Madam, Cudgels, Bear-baiting, Bull-
baiting, Bow and Arrow, Throwing at Cocks, Shuttle-*

20 'Fool Plough'—a harvest celebration in Yorkshire, 1814

cock, *Bowling, Quaits, Leaping, Wrestling, Pitching the Barre,* and *Ringing of Bells* a Recreation used in no other Countrey of the World.

Amongst these Cock-fighting seems to all Forreigners too *childish* and *unsuitable* for the *Gentry,* and for the Common People *Bull-baiting* and *Bear-baiting* seem too *cruel,* and for the Citizens *Foot-ball* very *uncivil, rude,* and *barbarous* within the City.

Joseph Strutt, in SPORTS AND PASTIMES OF THE PEOPLE OF ENGLAND (1801), *explained some of the games named by Chamberlayne.*

To play at this game [quoits], an iron pin, called a hob, is driven into the ground, within a few inches of the top; and at the distance of eighteen, twenty, or more yards, for the distance is optional, a second pin of iron is also made fast in a similar manner, and two or more persons, who are to contend for the victory, stand at one end of the iron marks and throw an equal number of quoits to the other, and the nearest of them to the hob are reckoned towards the game. . . . Formerly in the country, the rustics not having the round perforated quoits to play with, used horse-shoes, and in many places the quoit itself to this day is called a shoe. . . .

Tip-cat . . . is a rustic pastime well known in many parts of the kingdom. Its denomination is derived from a piece of wood called a cat, with which it is

21 *'Nor and Spell'—a variation of tip-cat played in the North*

played; the cat is about six inches in length and an inch and a half or two inches in diameter, and diminished from the middle to both the ends in the shape of a double cone. . . . When the cat is laid upon the ground the player with his cudgel strikes it smartly, it matters not at which end, and it will rise with a rotatory motion, high enough for him to beat it away as it falls, in the same manner as he would a ball. [The game] consists in making a large ring upon the ground, in the middle of which the striker takes his station; his business is to beat the cat over the ring. If he fails in so doing he is out, and another player takes his place; if he is successful he judges with his eye the distance the cat is driven . . . and calls for a number at pleasure to be scored towards his game: if the number demanded be found upon measurement to exceed the same number of lengths of the bludgeon, he is out; on the contrary, if it does not, he obtains his call. . . .

Throwing at Cocks was a very popular diversion, especially among the younger parts of the Community, and universally practised upon Shrove-tuesday. If the poor bird by chance had its legs broken, or was otherwise so lamed as not to be able to stand, the barbarous owners were wont to support it with sticks, in order to prolong the pleasure received from the

41

reiteration of its torment. The magistrates, greatly to their credit, have for some years past put a stop to this wicked custom, and at present it is nearly, if not entirely, discontinued in every part of the kingdom.

Bull-baiting

On 18 April, 1800, William Windham made a speech in Parliament in defence of bull-baiting, but his attitude was partly inspired by fear of the mob's reaction to a ban on it.

A great deal has lately been said respecting the state of the poor, and the hardships which they are suffering. But if they are really in the condition which is described, why should we set about to deprive them of the few enjoyments which are left to them. . . . The sport here, it must be confessed, is at the expence of an animal which is not by any means a party to the amusement; but it at the same time serves to cultivate the qualities of a certain species of dogs, which affords as much pleasure to their owners as greyhounds do to others. . . . It may be said, that in bull-baiting the labouring poor throw away their money, and lose their time, which they ought to devote to labour, and that thus they themselves may become chargeable to the rich. But surely, if there be any set of men who ought to be left at liberty to dispose of their money as they chose, it ought to be the industrious labourers. . . . In a bull-baiting a hedge may be broken down, or a field of grass trodden down; but what is that compared to the injury done by a pack of hounds, followed by horses and their riders, sweeping over fields and hedges without distinction? Accidents to the lookers-on do sometimes happen at bull-baiting; but I am sure that I have known more fatal accidents than ever happened from bull-baiting, arise in the county of Norfolk alone . . . by Quarrels between game-invaders and the game-preservers, some being killed

22 *Robert Owen's mills at New Lanark in Scotland, 1807. Owen treated his workers humanely and provided education for the children*

42

on the spot, and others hanged afterwards for the murders. . . .

Leisure in the Industrial Age

Robert Owen, writing his OBSERVATIONS ON THE EFFECT OF THE MANUFACTURING SYSTEM (1815), *had an explanation for the lack of constructive amusements among the working classes.*

In the manufacturing districts it is common for parents to send their children of both sexes at seven or eight years of age, in winter as well as summer, at six o'clock in the morning, sometimes of course in the dark, and occasionally amidst frost and snow, to enter the manufactories, which are often heated to a high temperature, and contain an atmosphere far from being the most favourable to human life, and in which all those employed in them very frequently continue until twelve o'clock at noon, when an hour is allowed for dinner, after which they return to remain, in a majority of cases, till eight o'clock at night.

The children now find they must labour incessantly for their bare subsistence; they have not been used to innocent, healthy, and rational amusements; they are not permitted the requisite time, if they had been previously accustomed to enjoy them. They know not what relaxation means, except by the actual cessation from labour. They are surrounded by others similarly circumstanced with themselves; and thus passing on from childhood to youth, they become gradually initiated, the young men in particular, but often the young females also, in the seductive pleasures of the pot-house and inebriation: for which their daily hard labour, want of better habits, and the general vacuity of their minds, tend to prepare them.

A Seaside Town

Sir George Head, in A HOME TOUR THROUGH THE MANUFACTURING DISTRICTS OF ENGLAND (1835), *found that there was still innocent fun to be had at festival time in factory towns, despite the general pattern of behaviour.*

Since I have undertaken to relate a part of the gaieties with which I mingled during the few days of my sojourn at Southport, I must add to the foregoing another rural festival, in the way of races and sports, celebrated on the sands. The ceremonial was duly announced some days before by large placards, printed and distributed, to give it publicity; by these it was set forth, that races would take place between donkeys, and the spavined old horses used in the bathing-machines; that men would hop in sacks, trundle wheelbarrows blindfold, chase a pig with a soaped tail; and that boys would climb a greased pole for a gold laced hat, and dip for pieces of drowned money in a bowl of treacle. . . .

Theatres and Music Halls

In his magazine, LONDON LABOUR AND THE LONDON POOR (1867), *Henry Mayhew set out to uncover the vices and miseries of the capital, but he studied the poorer classes in their lighter moments as well. At the music hall he found that romanticism and sentiment held little appeal for the young audience.*

On a good attractive night, the rush of costers to the 3*d*. gallery of the Coberg (better known as 'the Vic') is peculiar and almost awful.

The long zig-zag staircase that leads to the pay-box is crowded to suffocation at least an hour before the theatre is opened; but, on the occasion of a piece with a good murder in it, the crowd will frequently collect as early as 3 o'clock in the afternoon.

There are few grown-up men that go to the 'Vic' gallery. The generality of the visitors are lads from about twelve to three-and-twenty, and though a few black-faced sweeps or whitey-brown dustmen may be among the throng, the gallery audience consists mainly of coster-mongers. . . .

The 'Vic' gallery is not to be moved by touching sentiment. They prefer vigorous exercise to any

THE ROTUNDA, BLACKFRIAR'S ROAD.

emotional speech. . . . The dances and comic songs, between the pieces, are liked better than anything else. . . .

But the grand hit of the evening is always when a song is sung in which the entire gallery can join in chorus. . . .

Karl Baedeker's guide, LONDON AND ITS ENVIRONS (1900), *showed the importance of the theatres and music halls in London life.*

London possesses about 50 theatres and about

23 *A 'Penny Gaff', or unlicensed playhouse, where dumb-shows were performed. The audiences at these 'gaffs' were notoriously disorderly*

500 music-halls, which are visited by 325,000 people nightly or nearly 100,000,000 yearly. A visit to the whole of the theatres of London, which, however, could only be managed in the course of a prolonged sojourn, would give the traveller a capital insight into the social life of the people throughout all its gradations.

Use of Amenities

L. V. Sharp, writing the chapter on Leeds in SOCIAL CONDITIONS IN PROVINCIAL TOWNS (*edited by B. Bosanquet,* 1912), *found that the provision of public amenities did not solve the problems that Owen had recognised.*

A survey of the people's amusements would be full of instruction, but it would not always be pleasant reading. Leeds has left its people very much to themselves in this respect.

24 *The origins of feast days differed from area to area. The one pictured here commemorated the restoration of Charles II after the Puritan Revolution*

The capital expenditure of the corporation on parks has been a little over half a million, and this includes the purchase of Roundhay Park, which contains over 600 acres, and is certainly one of the finest parks in the provinces. It is, however, at least three miles from the slum areas of the city and has probably never been visited by the slum dwellers— though for that matter who ever sees slum children in a park? There are several small parks or 'moors', and some bare and desolate 'open spaces' are to be found in the most populous districts. . . . There is a Central Free Library and 27 branch libraries. . . .

There are two theatres, three or four music-halls,

RESTORATION-DAY (29TH OF MAY) AT UPTON-ON-SEVERN, WORCESTERSHIRE.

and some 'Picture Palaces'. . . .

The old 'Feasts' are still held annually, and in some districts the works close down for three or four days.

When all is said, the street remains the playground of the people, and the principal streets in the City of Leeds on Saturday night and Sunday should chasten the most hardened optimist. Vice there is—plenty; but almost worse than this the vacancy of mind which wanders up and down and *does nothing*. A jostling crowd mainly of young people physically and mentally unhealthy flows over the road. The problem of how to help the young citizen to recreate himself is growing more and more pressing.

Spectator Sports

Professional football and county cricket attracted large crowds in the third and fourth decades of this century. J. B. Priestley, in THE GOOD COMPANIONS (1929), *made the point that sport at second hand was for many people the only topic of interest in their lives.*

Thirty-five thousand men and boys have just seen what most of them call 't'United' play Bolton Wanderers. Many of them should never have been there at all. It would not be difficult to prove by statistics and those mournful little budgets (How a Man May Live—or rather, avoid death—on Thirty-five shillings a Week) that seem to attract some minds, that these fellows could not afford the entrance fee. When some mills are only working half the week and the others not at all, a shilling is a respectable sum of money.

. . . For a shilling the Bruddersford United A.F.C. offered you Conflict and Art . . . it turned you into a member of a new community, all brothers together for an hour and a half, for not only had you escaped from the clanking machinery of this lesser life, from work, wages, rent, doles, sick pay, insurance cards, nagging wives, ailing children, bad bosses, idle workmen, but you had excaped with most of your mates and your neighbours, with half the town. . . . Moreover, it offered you more than a shilling's worth of material for talk during the rest of the week. A man who had missed the last home match of 't'United' had to enter social life on tiptoe in Bruddersford.

CHAPTER THREE

THE REACTION AGAINST POVERTY

In times of severe hardship, the poor would give vent to their desperation by forming violent mobs and attacking the immediate cause of their distress. Alternatively they would be found flocking to the banners of a protest movement, not because the cause held a direct appeal for them, but because it provided an outlet for their frustrations.

As trade unions developed, grievances could be aired— and resolved—by more peaceful methods (though violent strikes did occur); and once the unions became involved in politics, working-class influence began to affect the government's social policies. Inevitably, however, there was a strong reaction from those who felt their interests were threatened by the unions' increasing power in politics and industry. When the economic troubles of the twenties and thirties brought mass unemployment across the country, reactionary industrialists and politicians drew some consolation from the fact that the consequent loss of bargaining power reduced the union movement to a low ebb.

Destructive Activities

When enclosure threatened their livelihood, the villagers of the seventeenth century often turned out in force. The victims of enclosure riots appealed to the Privy Council for appropriate action to be taken, and part of one such appeal is reproduced below.

April 5 1631. Information of Robert Bridges of Hillere Land in Mailescott, in the parish of Bicknor, in the Forest of Dean, co. Gloucester. On 25 March 500 persons with two drums, two colours, and a fife, assembled themselves together armed with guns and pikes, and threw down near 100 perches of ditching newly made, and shot off pieces charged with bullets against deponent's house, which they threatened to pull down if he spake a word. They committed also many other acts of riot, ending by proclaiming with an "O yes!" that if deponent made the like work against Mayday next, they would be ready to do him the like service again.

[CALENDAR OF STATE PAPERS, DOMESTIC SERIES, 1631-33]

From 1740 (*when the following account appeared in* THE GENTLEMAN'S MAGAZINE) *until the end of the eighteenth century the price of bread was generally very high. Bakers and millers bore the brunt of the angry mobs' displeasure.*

July 7. A Rabble at *Norwich* began to be tumultuous, and affix'd a Note on the Door of every Baker in the City, in these Words, *Wheat at sixteen Shillings a Comb.* Upon this the Court met at the Hall in the Market-place, and call'd a Guard of Dragoons, and Dispersed printed Advertisements, to inform the Multitude that they were determin'd, to the utmost

25 *A print showing a bread riot in Stockport, 1842. The Cheshire Yeomanry had to be called in to restore order*

of their Power, to put in Execution the Proclamation of the Lords Justices for preventing the Exportation of Corn. About 8 in the evening the Mayor committed 3 or 4 disorderly Fellows to Prison, which so incensed the Mob that they broke open the Prison and released their Companions, and still growing more furious, provok'd some to fire among them, whereby 3 Men, 2 Women, and a Boy were killed, and many more dangerously wounded.

The new machines of the Industrial Revolution, some capable of doing the work of fifty men or more, seemed to threaten large-scale redundancy, particularly in the textile industries. To protect their jobs men destroyed the power-driven looms and frames which were creating the factory system and displacing their cottage industry.

Josiah Wedgwood, the potter, described the following incident in a letter to Thomas Bentley, 9 October, 1779.

On the same day in the afternoon a capital engine or mill in the manner of Arcrites [Arkwright's] and in which he is a partner, near Chorley, was attacked, but from its peculiar position, they could approach it by one passage only, and this circumstance enabled the owner, with the assistance of a few neighbours, to repulse the enemy and preserve the mill for that time. Two of the mob were shot dead upon the spot, one drowned and several wounded. Accordingly they spent all Sunday and Monday morning in collecting firearms and ammunition and melting their pewter dishes into bullets. They were now joined by the Duke of Bridgewater's colliers and others, to the number, we were told, of eight thousand, and marched by beat of drum and with colours flying to the mill where they met with a repulse on Saturday. They found Sir Richard Clayton guarding the place with fifty armed invalids, but this handful were by no means a match for enraged thousands, so they contented themselves (the invalids) with looking on, while the mob completely destroyed a set of mills valued at £10,000. This was Monday's employment. On Tuesday morning we heard their drums at about two miles' distance from Bolton, a little before we left the place, and their professed design was to take Bolton, Manchester and Stockport on their way to Cromford, and to destroy all the engines not only in these places, but throughout all England.

The ANNUAL REGISTER *of 1811 reported on the activities of the Luddites, an extensive machine-breaking organisation which originated in Nottinghamshire.*

On November the 10th, a number of weavers assembling near Nottingham, began forcibly to enter houses in which were frames of this kind, and destroy them. On the 11th they appeared before the house of a manufacturer at Bulwell, which was barricaded by the owner, who had also armed men in its defence. On attempting to break in, the mob was fired at, and one person killed. This roused them to fury, and in increasing numbers they renewed their attack, made an entry, the family having escaped to save their lives, and burnt everything in the house. This act seemed a signal for more extensive outrages . . .

The rioters assumed the name of *Luddites,* and acted under the authority of an imaginary *Captain Ludd,* which name seems to have signified not one individual, but a secret committee of management. The spirit of tumult spread into the neighbouring counties of Derby and Leicester, in the manufacturing parts of which many frames were destroyed . . .

From the 1830s to the 1880s uncertain markets had an adverse effect on agriculture, and farmers passed their troubles on to their employees by paying low wages. Agricultural labourers had no effective organisation to combat these cuts, so they became a depressed class whose outbursts of discontent took the form of rick-burning and the destruction of crops. James Caird, in ENGLISH AGRICULTURE 1850-51, *wrote of disturbances in Cambridgeshire.*

In any district of England in which we have yet been, we have not heard the farmers speak in a tone of greater discouragement than here. Their wheat crop, last year, was of inferior quality, the price unusually low, and, to add to this, their live stock and crop are continually exposed to the match of the prowling incendiary. Such a state of matters is unendurable, and not a little discreditable to the police arrangements of the district. To get rid of so great an evil we should consider the rent of the county well expended in setting a watch on every corn rick in it, if no less effectual means of prevention can be adopted. To say that, in a district within fifty miles of London, property is so insecure ana even life in some degree of hazard, is to tell us of a country in a semi-barbarous state. A man might as well expose his life to the risk of a shot from a Tipperary assassin, as live, like a Cambridgeshire farmer, in constant apprehension of incendiarism.

Whatever the cause, the evil itself must be put down. We were assured that no considerate or kindly treatment of his labourers on the part of an individual farmer was any protection to him. Fires break out indiscriminately among all—the kindest and most large hearted as often as the most selfish and narrow minded. A few bad fellows in a district are believed to do all the mischief, and bring discredit on the whole rural population. The fact of its existence argues discontent among the labouring class, for which the low rate of wages may in some degree account, 7s. to 8s. a week being the current rate. Cottage rents are from £2. to as much, in some parishes, as £4 or £5, so that a labourer on 7s. a week has little to spare for the necessaries of life after paying his landlord 1s. 6d. or 2s. out of it. Labourers are fairly employed.

The Search for a Cause

Horace Walpole (1717-97), the shrewd, witty gossip and man of letters, saw many examples of mob violence during the uneasy eighteenth century. He lived through disturbances over the Excise Bill of 1733, the Gin Act of 1736, the refusal to allow Wilkes to take his seat in Parliament in 1768, and the granting of toleration to Catholics. In all these cases the mob's excesses owed much to the desperation created by extreme poverty.

Walpole's letter to Sir Horace Mann, dated 5 June 1780, described the opening stages in the Gordon Riots. It was obvious to him that the mob would take control over their weak and ineffectual leader.

. . . Lord George Gordon, gave notice to the House of Commons last week, that he would, on Friday, bring in the petition of the Protestant Association;

26 *Horace Walpole, the son of Sir Robert Walpole (Prime Minister 1721-42)*

and he openly declared to his disciples, that he would not carry it unless *a noble army of martyrs, not fewer than forty thousand,* would accompany him. Forty thousand, led by such a lamb, were more likely to prove butchers than victims; and so, in good truth, they were very near being . . . Early on Friday morning the conservators of the Church of England assembled in St George's Fields to encounter the dragon, the old serpent, and marched in lines of six and six—about thirteen thousand only, as they were computed—with a petition as long as the procession, which the apostle himself presented; but, though he had given out most Christian injunctions for peaceable behaviour, he did everything in his power to promote a massacre. He demanded immediate repeal of toleration, told Lord North he could have him torn to pieces, and, running every minute to the door or windows, bawled to the populace that Lord North would give no redress, and that now this member, now that, was speaking against them.

27 *Gordon was a foolish idealist who exposed London to riots lasting for four days in his campaign against 'the Catholic menace'*

Countess Ossory was given a second-hand account of the Gordon Riots in Walpole's letter of 8 June 1780, which showed that fear of Catholicism was not uppermost in the minds of the rioters.

I do not know whether to call the horrors of the night greater or less than I thought. My printer, who has been out all night, and on the spots of action, says, not above a dozen were killed at the Royal Exchange, some few elsewhere; at the King's Bench, he does not know how many; but in other respects the calamities are dreadful. He saw many houses set on fire, women and children screaming, running out of doors with what they could save, and knocking one another down with their loads in the confusion. Barnard's Inn is burnt, and some houses, mistaken for Catholic. Kirgate says most of the rioters are apprentices, and plunder and drink have been their chief objects, and both women and men are still lying dead drunk about the streets: brandy is preferable to enthusiasm. I trust many more troops will arrive today. What families ruined! What wretched wives and mothers! What public disgrace!—ay! and where, and when, and how will all this confusion end! And what shall we be when it is concluded? I remember the Excise and the Gin Act, and the rebels at Derby, and Wilkes's interlude, and the French at Plymouth; or I should have a very bad memory; but I never till last night saw London and Southwark in flames!

Between 1836 and 1848 Chartism flourished as a great working-class movement for parliamentary reform, and its advocates clearly outlined the benefits which they hoped to achieve for the poorer classes. Even so, powerful support was only won during the years of bad harvest or trade depression—1839, 1842, 1846, and 1848. William Lovett and John Collins, two Chartist leaders, wrote CHARTISM; A NEW ORGANIZATION OF THE PEOPLE *while they were in gaol in 1840. The extract below defends the first demand of the 'People's Charter'—votes for all.*

The supposition that Universal Suffrage would give the working classes a *preponderating power* in the House of Commons, is not borne out by the experience of other countries. They are far from possessing such a power even in America, where wealth and rank have far less influence than with us, and where the exercise of the suffrage for more than half

a century have given them opportunities to get their rights better represented than they are. But *wealth* with them, as with us, will always maintain *an undue influence*, till the people are *morally* and *politically* instructed; then, indeed, will wealth secure *its just and proper influence*, and not, as at present, stand in opposition to the claims of industry, intellect, merit, freedom, and happiness. But the great advantages of the suffrage in the interim will be these: it will afford the people general and superior *means* of instruction; it will awaken and concentrate human intellect to remove the evils of social life; and will compel the representatives of the people to redress grievances, improve laws, and provide means of happiness in proportion to the enlightened desires of public opinion. Such indeed are the results we anticipate from the passing of the PEOPLE'S CHARTER.

Thomas Cooper, in his autobiography (written in 1872), described a Chartist meeting held at Hanley, one of the 'Pottery Towns', in 1842. He knew how accounts of misery and exploitation could stir his audience.

I took for a text the sixth commandment: "Thou shalt do no murder"—After we had sung Bramwich's hymn 'Britannia's sons, though slaves ye be,' and I had offered a short prayer . . . I showed that low wages for wretched agricultural labourers, and the brutal ignorance in which generation after generation they were left by the landlords, was a violation of the precept, "Thou shalt do no murder."

I asserted that the attempt to lessen the wages of toilers underground, who were in hourly and momentary danger of their lives, and to disable them from getting the necessary food for themselves and families, were violations of the precept, "Thou shalt do no murder."

I declared that all who were instrumental in maintaining the system of labour which reduced poor

28 *William Lovett, the first leader of the Chartist movement*

stockingers to the starvation I had witnessed in Leicester,—and which was witnessed among the poor handloom weavers of Lancashire, and poor nailmakers of the Black Country—were violating the precept, "Thou shalt do no murder."

And now the multitude shouted; and their looks told of vengeance—but I went on, for I felt as if I could die on the spot in fulfilling a great duty—the exposure of human wrong and consequent human suffering. My strength was great at that time, and my voice could be heard, like the peal of a trumpet, even to the verge of a crowd composed of thousands.

[*The next day Cooper chaired a meeting at Hanley where the resolution was passed 'That all labour cease until the People's Charter becomes the law of the land'. He had earlier told the meeting that 'Peace, Law, and Order' should be their motto; nevertheless the resolution sparked off a riot in which magistrates' houses were burnt down, and cavalry opened fire. One man was killed, and scores arrested.*]

Times were hard in the 1930s, but the poor retained sufficient integrity to reject Fascism as the answer to their problems. Those who wanted an outlet in violence might find it in fighting pitched battles against the 'Blackshirts'.

The Fascist meeting at Olympia last night suffered from continuous interruptions, and the interrupters suffered heavily at the hands of the blackshirted stewards, male and female. The meeting began 40 minutes late because demonstrations outside obstructed, and, as Sir Oswald Mosley said, intimidated some of the people on their way in. It proceeded easily for the first 10 minutes before the Socialists made their first move. Another five minutes passed before the next clash occurred. After that strife broke out in different parts of the hall at about three minute intervals . . .

It was a strangely mixed audience. A very large

29 *A scene during the Fascist demonstration in London, 1936. Moseley's blackshirts received rough treatment from the East-enders*

proportion were onlookers—people of middle-age who wore neither black shirt nor badge; people with a tired expression of eye and wrinkled brows; some of the people who bore the strain of the war and the cost of the peace.

There seemed to be few people of the professional classes. Few were well enough dressed to suggest affluence. They were rather those who have tired of passing through difficult times in which hope has been strained. And they seemed to be looking for the reason beneath this resurgence of youthful enthusiasm and militant spirit, lest they should have missed a chance of deliverance which these in their inexperience had miraculously found. In so big a crowd there was comparatively little cheering.

The impression one gained was that the enquirers, who feared they had become back numbers, had neither found the secret nor caught the enthusiasm. Before the speech was over they began to trickle away in little streams towards the exits.

[THE TIMES, 8 June 1934]

Trade Unions

Combinations of workers were illegal between 1800 and 1824, and workmen could only meet together for the purpose of presenting petitions. Under cover, however, they were preparing themselves for the day when they could do more than make polite requests to their employers.

AT a MEETING of the FRAMEWORK-KNITTERS, held at the VAUXHALL, Mr. THORPE, in the Chair.

THE FOLLOWING RESOLUTIONS WERE UNANIMOUSLY AGREED TO
Resolved,

That it appears to this Meeting, that the great and lamentable depression of Wages has, principally arisen, not from a desire, on the part of the Hosiers, to reduce the Stocking Maker to that misery and wretchedness which he now endures, but from a Competition to undersell each other in the Market.

2d—That the reducing of the Wages of the Mechanic, at all times to be deprecated as injurious to the peace, happiness, and prosperity of the great body of the People, is peculiarly so at the present moment, when the first necessary of life is exhorbitantly high. . .

4th—That the wages of the Stocking Maker are now reduced so low, that he cannot obtain the first Necessaries of Life, by the most patient Industry, and unwearied Application to the Duties of his Calling; and those cries of his Children for Bread, which pierce his Heart, he can only stop by the most painful chastisement.

5th—That an ADVANCE of our WAGES, to an Amount which could enable us to Live by our Labour, while it would not be felt by the Consumer, would make us cheerful, contented, and happy.

6th—That in proportion as the Reduction of Wages makes the great Body of People *poor and wretched*, in the same proportion must the consumption of our Manufactures be lessened . . .

10th—that a Deputation be appointed to wait upon the Hosiers, to request them to call an early Meeting, to take into their consideration the Distress arising from the great Reduction of Prices.

JOHN THORPE, *Chairman*
[LEICESTER JOURNAL, 7 February 1817]

Robert Owen was the first to envisage a wider role for unions, and to form a national amalgamation, but his experiment was short-lived.

XLVI. That, although the design of the Union is, in the first instance, to raise the wages of the workmen, or prevent any further reduction therein, and to diminish the hours of labour, the great and ultimate object of it must be to establish the paramount rights of Industry and Humanity, by instituting such measures as shall effectually prevent the ignorant, idle, and useless part of society from having that undue control over the fruits of our toil, which,

30 *Robert Owen (1771-1858) by E. Morley. Although a factory owner, Owen was in the forefront of movements aimed at benefiting the working classes*

through the agency of a vicious money system, they at present possess; and that, consequently, the Unionists should lose no opportunity of mutually encouraging and assisting each other in bringing about A DIFFERENT STATE OF THINGS, in which the really useful and intelligent part of society only shall have the direction of its affairs, and in which well-directed industry and virtue shall meet their just distinction and reward, and vicious idleness its merited contempt and destitution.

[RULES OF THE GRAND NATIONAL CONSOLIDATED TRADES UNIONS, 1834]

A well-organised strike was a powerful instrument, but strikers were subject to laws against conspiracy all through the nineteenth century; and employers hit back with lockouts and the use of non-union labour—as the ANNUAL REGISTER *of 1872 noted with approval.*

The numerous strikes that have occurred during the year have produced general anxiety by the formidable nature of their possible results, and by the extension of the system to classes which had hitherto abstained from combination . . .

At the most active season of the year, early in the summer, the workmen in the London building trade struck for a reduction of the hours of labour, and consequently almost all building operations were suspended for two or three of the best months of the year. The battle was begun by the masons and the joiners, who presented memorials to the employers for 'nine hours, and ninepence per hour'. The strike of the joiners against two large firms belonging to the Masters' Association produced a lock-out on the 17th of June, throwing out of employment the men in the other branches who had taken no part in the movement—the painters, plasterers, bricklayers, metal workers, and labourers . . .

Shortly afterwards the Stokers in the employment of several of the London Gas Companies suddenly abandoned their employment at the dictation of a recently formed union . . . The Chartered Gas Company, which was exceptionally ill-treated by the men in its employ, summarily and permanently dismissed all the strikers, 1400 in number, and five of the leaders of the strike were indicted for conspiracy, and tried at the Central Criminal Court before Justice Brett, who summed up heavily against them, and on their being convicted on the counts that charged conspiracy, sentenced them to twelve months' imprisonment.

A Wider Role for Unions

From 1869 onwards unions were backing their own candidates for Parliament, and eventually formed a party of their own—in 1900 the Trades Union Congress founded the Labour Representation Committee, out of

31 *A violent strike near Sheffield, 1870. The pictures show stages in an attack by miners upon non-unionists*

TANKERSLEY PIT

TANKERSLEY FARM

WESTWOOD STATION

POLICE CHARGING THE MOB

*which grew the Labour Party. Ben Tillett, the dockers'
leader, in a speech to the Labour Party Annual Conference of 1907, objected to the presence of the Fabians
in the labour movement who were not trade unionists.*

. . . The Trade Union official who did something
towards adding a shilling to the wage and to put more
food upon the table of the worker was doing a greater
work than sentimental men talking about theories.
Trade Unionism was a class-conscious movement;
it was the only class-conscious movement. Its
general tendency was to become class-conscious, not
only in dealing with employers, but in a wider
political sense. If the Dockers could organize, where
there was practically an average of 50 per cent
constantly employed; if the General Labourers could
organize, then he looked upon these literary, clever,
well-educated men attached to the Movement as the

greatest black-legs if they could not organize in
their own professions. He knew it was not considered
right for a salaried man to be as common as a wage-
earner. Many of these eloquent and clever men
attached to the Movement were Trade Unionists,
but some of them were not. If they were not, then
they were against them.

*The dock strike of 1911 disrupted the country, and
ended in success for the huge Transport Workers
Federation. This was a victory for industrial unionism—'one industry one union'. Winston Churchill,
Home Secretary at the time, wrote a worried memoran-
dum on the extent of the trouble.*

There is grave unrest in the country. Port after
port is called out. The police and the military are
asked for at place after place. Fresh outbreaks continuously occur and will go on. The railways are not
sound. Transport workers everywhere are getting to
know their strength, while the 'hooligan' element are
causing riots: and those conversant of labour matters
in practice anticipate grave upheaval. Serious crises

32 *Wigan miners listening to a union official during a
strike in 1921. The miners were in continuous conflict
with their bosses at this time, and it was their grievances
that ushered in the General Strike*

have been in recent years, and very often lately, surmounted only by a narrow margin of safety and now specially a new force has arisen in trades unionism, whereby the power of the old leaders has proved quite ineffective, and the sympathetic strike on a wide scale is prominent. Shipping, coal, railways, dockers etc etc are all uniting and breaking out at once. The 'general strike' policy is a factor which must be dealt with . . .

On 14 August 1911 Churchill sent a telegram to the King to inform him that the army was being called in. The communication illustrates the attitudes which ruled out compromise and co-operation.

Mr Secretary Churchill with great respect. He has received the following report from Head Constable, Liverpool. The situation is no better, rather worse. The dockers have not gone back to work and the shipowners have declared a general lockout from this afternoon to apply to all dock workers. There is a good deal of riotous disturbance particularly in the Irish quarter and a squadron of the Scots Greys is

33 *Although there were one or two outbreaks of violence, the strikers of 1926 were generally on good terms with the authorities. The picture above shows a football match between strikers and police*

proceeding there—a body of Warwickshires will follow. The riot last night started with the hooligans not strikers but was quickly taken up by the latter . . . [*Randolph Churchill,* WINSTON S. CHURCHILL, *Companion Volume II,* 1969]

The General Strike

Many feared that the General Strike of 1926 heralded the 'red revolution', but after nine relatively bloodless days it was abandoned; the unions had overstepped themselves. Stanley Baldwin, Prime Minister at the time, made a placatory speech on the subject at Chippenham in June 1926, but a year later he pushed through the Trade Disputes Act, which banned sympathetic strikes.

There was no doubt in my mind—and I am going to give you my views—that there were responsible and respected trade union leaders who assented with reluctance and with anxiety to the telegrams ordering the General Strike, and in the hope that somehow or other the consequences of their action would be avoided. Some of them saw and believed, without reason in my view, but also genuinely from their point of view, that if the miners had to concede anything in wages or in hours the industries which they represented would be, in their own language, attacked next, and they were determined to ward off that attack . . . But there were other leaders who . . . regarded any such attempt as a chance of bringing off or aiding what is called the social revolution. It is certain, too, that however much you may call or believe the General Strike to be industrial, the results are political and social. It is a great tribute to the good qualities of the strikers, who are our own people, that they showed that sense of discipline and restraint in obedience to their instructions. . . . I recognize the courage that it took on the part of the leaders who had taken a false step to recede from that position unconditionally, as they did on May 12. It took a good deal more courage than it takes their critics now, who are blaming them for not going straight on, whatever happened. But if that strike showed solidarity, sympathy with the miners— whatever you like—it showed something else far greater. It proved the stability of the whole fabric of our country, and to the amazement of the world not a shot was fired.

[*Stanley Baldwin*, OUR INHERITANCE, 1928]

Protest Marches

Hunger marches, peacefully conducted, seemed to be the sole means of publicising the plight of the inhabitants of depressed areas during the 1930s. The unemployed, of course, had no bargaining power. Ellen Wilkinson, MP for Jarrow, wrote of the famous Jarrow March in THE TOWN THAT WAS MURDERED (1939).

When Parliament reassembled there were two petitions to be presented. The one, bound in the book we had carried across England, of nearly 12,000 signatures. The other, of 68,500 from the towns on Tyneside, presented by Sir Nicholas Grattan-Doyle, the senior member for Newcastle. The Jarrow petition stated that the town had been passing through a long period of industrial depression without parallel in its history . . . its shipyards closed, its steel-works denied the right to re-open. Whereas formerly 8000 workers were employed, only 100 were now at work, and those on temporary schemes. 'The town cannot be left derelict, and therefore your petitioners humbly pray that His Majesty's Government and this honourable House will realise the urgent need that work should be provided for the town without delay.'

. . . The actual presentation at best could only be a gesture. What mattered more, in a practical sense, was the crowded meeting of members of all parties in the biggest committee room in the House of Commons to hear the Labour Mayor, Councillor Thompson, the Liberal ex-Mayor, Councillor Dodds, and the Town Clerk state the case about the ship-yard and the steelworks. There was a dramatic moment when the Mayor held up his chain of office. 'This chain,' he said, 'was given to the town by Sir Charles Mark Palmer. Its links form a cable, its badge is an anchor . . . symbols in gold of the cables and anchors of the thousand ships we built at Jarrow. Now, owing to National Shipbuilders' Security, Ltd., the Jarrow shipyard is closed. Ships for Britain's food and her defence will be made in that yard no more. God grant the time may not come when you members of Parliament will have need to regret that you allowed the scrapping of this great national asset in the interest of the private profit of a bank's shareholders.'

34 *The Jarrow Marchers at Bedford, lining up for corned beef and potatoes*

CHAPTER FOUR

THE WORK OF THE PHILANTHROPISTS

The material and spiritual welfare of the poor has always been regarded as a Christian responsibility; thus inevitably most philanthropists were religiously orientated until recent times. Compassionate and public-spirited churchmen, reacting against the manifestations of poverty, expended their time and money to serve those in need, sometimes alone, sometimes by forming societies or founding institutions. The most successful were those who tackled specific problems in depth, and gained sufficient experience and understanding to take practical and realistic action. These were the true pioneers, and where they led governments eventually followed, especially in caring for the children of the poor.

The Early Quakers

The seventeenth-century Quakers provided food for the poor who approached them, but their exhortations and plans for a programme of good works were either too general or too idealistic to be effective. George Fox, in his pamphlet ADVICE AND WARNING TO THE MAGISTRATES OF LONDON (1657), *appealed to a sense of Christian duty but had no constructive proposals to put forward.*

Would not a little out of your Abundance and Superfluity maintain these poor Children, Halt, Lame and Blind, or set them to Work that can work, and they that cannot; find a Place of Relief for them: Would not that be a Grace to You? That else will be a Disgrace, and shew that you want the *Wisdom of God* to order the Creation.

Him that turns his Ear from hearing the Cry of the Poor, the Lord will not regard, he that despiseth the Poor, despiseth his Maker.

This is the Word of the LORD GOD *to You all, and a Charge to you all in the* PRESENCE *of the* LORD GOD.

See all the Poor, the Blind, Lame, the Widows, the Fatherless, that cry up and down your Streets for Bread.

That these be taken up and provided for, and they that can work, that they be set to it, and that they that cannot, that they may be looked to, that there may be a good Savour in your Streets, that the Lord may come with a Blessing upon you, and give you an Increase double another Way.

Then you shew the Fruits of true Religion, and Works of Charity, and the Fruits of Love, and the Fruits of the Spirit.

They regard not their own Flesh, they regard not their Creator, that regard not their Fellow Creature, that He created; who created the one as well as the other.

John Bellers was a prominent Quaker of the next generation, and in PROPOSALS FOR RAISING A COLLEGE OF INDUSTRY (1696) *he glibly claimed that workhouses could operate at a profit.*

Shewing how the Rich may gain, the Poor maintain themselves, and their Children be educated, by being incoporated as a College of all Sorts of useful Trades, that shall work one for another, without other Relief. I suppose 300 in a Colledge, to work the usual Time or Task as abroad, and what any doth more to be paid for it, to encourage Industry.

One Hundred and Fifty two of all Trades, I comput is sufficient to find all Necessaries for 300, and therefore what Manufacture the other 148 make, will be profit for the Founders.

Charitable Subscriptions

Most people with charitable intentions did not involve themselves directly in the service of the poor, but provided money for such service. Robert Nelson, a key figure in the Society for the Promotion of Christian Knowledge during Anne's reign, set out to woo these people in order to finance the society's various charities.
. . . when the good Spirit of GOD hath disposed their Minds to contribute towards the Spiritual and Temporal Wants of the Ignorant and Necessitous, when their Hearts are as ready to supply the Poor, as

their Estates are plentiful to furnish Materials for it, they may be at a Loss for fit and proper Objects to exercise their Charity upon; for their Condition of Life sets them at a Distance from the lamentable Complaints which the Inferior Part of Mankind labour under; and the Way and Manner of Employing their Time, renders them uncapable of Performing their Alms-Deeds to the *best Advantage:* Therefore I thought it might be of great Use to facilitate their doing Good, to collect together all those several WAYS and METHODS which are now carrying on, to relieve the temporal Necessities of our Neighbour, and to furnish besides, the Poor with all those necessary Means of Instruction in *ChristianKnowledge*, as might tend to make them bear their hard Circumstances with Patience and Resignation to the Will of GOD, as well as to render them meet to be made Partakers of the Inheritance of the Saints in Light.
[AN ADDRESS TO PERSONS OF QUALITY AND ESTATE, 1715]

Sickness in the midst of poverty and squalor makes a dramatic impact on the eyes of the social observer, and hospitals were among the earliest of the charitable institutions founded on public subscriptions. Many of them were founded by secular societies. THE GENTLEMAN'S MAGAZINE *of 1747 recounted the origins of the London Infirmary.*
The LONDON INFIRMARY, For charitably relieving all sick and diseased poor, more especially manufacturers, seamen in merchants service, their wives and children.

THIS INFIRMARY was set on foot in the year 1740, by the voluntary subscription of several worthy noblemen, merchants, and others, to relieve a further number of those unhappy objects that daily offered themselves more than could be received by the hospitals then in being. How necessary this undertaking was, has since been confirmed by experience, no less than 30,000 patients having benefited by it in about six years, which would appear almost incredible, were it not considered, that this charity is extended to all nations and religions.

In a sermon of the Bishop of Worcester's, it is taken notice of in the following manner:

'These charitable doors are always open; open at every hour of every day; and open to every sufferer, how low soever reduced. None can be too poor and friendless to be relieved within these hospitable walls, no expence, no charge at their admission, nor any security required against future contingencies.'

Charity Schools

Mrs Sarah Trimmer, virtuous rather than kindly, was a strong supporter of organisations which provided care and education for pauper children, though she wanted these children to recognise and keep to their station in life. The following extract is from her book REFLECTIONS UPON THE EDUCATION OF CHILDREN IN CHARITY SCHOOLS (1792), *and shows the limitations of eighteenth-century thinking in this field.*

The objection against giving learning to the poor, lest it raise them above their situation, is completely obviated by making such learning as general as possible; for then it ceases to give pre-eminence, or to be a distinction, and must eventually qualify all better to fill their respective stations in society: and nothing could be thought of so well calculated to diffuse a moderate and useful share of learning among the lower order of people, as these schools . . .

Charity Schools hold out such superior advantages in some respects, as to give them a decided pre-eminence over all the subsisting establishments for gratuitous instruction, as the money collected for them is usually sufficient to afford clothing to the children, as well as learning; and in many Charity Schools the children are entirely maintained in the house, and some of them afterwards apprenticed to trades and manufactures.

But *Sunday Schools* and *Schools of Industry*, though the emoluments of the children are less, are of equal importance with the above institutions, as they afford instruction to unlimited numbers of children, who could not be admitted into *Charity Schools* . . .

Elizabeth Fry

Mrs Elizabeth Fry, a Quaker minister, was a remarkably active reformer. Apart from bringing up a large family she was a tireless social worker, and under her leadership women's philanthropic societies flourished. Her chief claim to fame lay in the field of prison reform, but she was also actively involved in founding schools, shelters for the homeless, and aid societies for beggars. The passage below describes some of her earlier charitable activities.

In establishing herself at Plashet [in 1811], Mrs

35 *Elizabeth Fry (1780-1845) by S. Drummond*

Fry had formed various plans for the benefit of her poorer neighbours, which she gradually brought into action. One of her early endeavours was to establish a girls' school for the Parish of East Ham; of which Plashet is a hamlet . . .

The bodily wants of the poor, especially in cases of sickness or accident, claimed her careful attention. There was a depot of callico and flannels always ready, besides outer garments, and a roomy closet well supplied with drugs. In very hard winters, she had soup boiled in an outhouse, in such quantities, as to supply hundreds of poor people with a nourishing meal . . .

. . . There was another class of persons who claimed the attentions of the ladies of the British Society at this meeting [in 1824]. The vicious and neglected little girls, so numerous in London, early hardened in crime, who, whether they had or had not been imprisoned, had no chance of reformation at home;

36 *Similar in concept to Mrs Fry's School of Discipline, the Philanthropic Society's farm at Redhill, opened in 1849, housed young male offenders and prepared them for eventual emigration. Note the prominent chapel*

yet were too young to be placed with advantage in any existing asylum. Before the next anniversary, a School of Discipline, for the reception of such children was opened at Chelsea, where, withdrawn from their former associates, they might be trained to orderly and virtuous habits. The idea first occurred to Mrs Fry, when conversing in the yard at Newgate, with her friend, Mrs Benjamin Shaw, on the extreme difficulty of disposing of some very juvenile prisoners about to be discharged. She then begged Mrs Shaw to consider the subject and to draw up some plan for the purpose . . .

[*K. and C. Fry*, MEMOIRS OF THE LIFE OF ELIZABETH FRY, 1847]

LORD SHAFTESBURY VISITING THE COAL MINES OF THE BLACK COUNTRY, 1840-42

37 *Mainly because of Shaftesbury's effort, children and women were banned from working in the mines in 1842*

Lord Shaftesbury

Lord Ashley, better known as Lord Shaftesbury (he inherited the title in 1851), was directly involved in various charities concerned with the children of the poor, but his main importance lay in his parliamentary campaigns for social legislation—he was a direct link between philanthropy and government. His article 'Infant Labour', which appeared in the QUARTERLY REVIEW *of December 1840, illustrated the extent to which Ashley was influenced by Christian motives.*

Damp and unhealthy substrata, left altogether without drainage; frail tenements, low and confined, without conveniences or ventilation; close alleys and no supply of water: all these things overtopped by the *ne plus ultra* of rent, reward the contractor and devour the inhabitants. Emerging from these lairs of filth and disorder; the young workers, 'rising early and late taking rest', go forth that they may toil through fifteen, nay seventeen relentless hours, in sinks and abysses . . .

Let your laws, we say to Parliament, assume the proper functions of law, protect those for whom neither wealth, nor station, nor age, have raised a bulwark against tyranny: but above all, open your treasury, erect churches, send forth the ministers of religion; reverse the conduct of the enemy of mankind, and sow wheat among the tares—all hopes are groundless, all legislation weak, all conservatism nonsense, without this alpha and omega of policy.

In speech to Parliament (reported in the ILLUSTRATED LONDON NEWS *of 12 April 1851) Ashley pursued his campaign against the squalor which bred vice—but his Bill was unsuccessful.*

Lord Ashley moved for leave to bring in a bill to encourage the construction of lodging houses for the working classes. The noble Lord referred to several documents to show the extent to which fever and other complaints prevailed in the badly-ventilated rooms in which the lower classes of the people reside in the densely-populated districts of the metropolis and other large towns. The accommodation for the migratory portion of the population was still more detestable. To remedy such a deplorable state of things he proposed the adoption of a bill precisely similar to the Baths and Wash-house Bill, which had produced such immense benefits to the working classes. A majority of two-thirds of the parishioners should have the power of bringing the bill into operation in their parish; after which they would have the power of constructing proper houses to correct the evils they complained of, and also to sell those houses, should they at any time become unnecessary. The houses to be built on the plan of the model lodging-houses, which were found to be amply remunerative, at rents rather less than those paid for the filthy and ill-ventilated rooms now occupied by labourers. While the physical condition of the people was so low, it would be impossible to expect to raise their moral condition . . .

The Abuse of Charity

There were pitfalls for those with charitable intentions; indiscriminate donations could encourage weaknesses such as those referred to in the evidence given by Rev Whitwell Elwin for the REPORT ON THE SANITARY CONDITIONS OF THE LABOURING POPULATION (1842).

I was lately informed by a master tailor of Bath that one of his men, who had earned £3 a-week at piece-work for years, had never within his knowledge possessed table, chairs, or bedding. I found the

38 *The Prince Consort sponsored a scheme to improve workers' living conditions, and paid for this home himself. It accommodated four families*

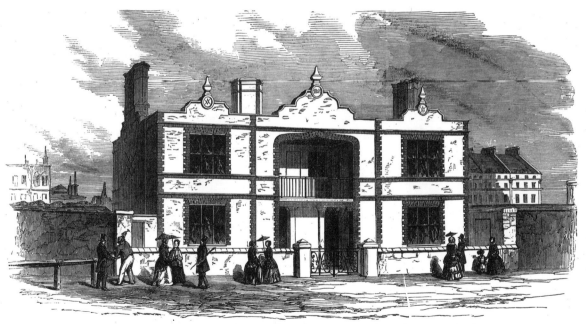

PRINCE ALBERT'S MODEL LODGING-HOUSE.

39 *A Ragged School in London, 1846*

statement on examination to be strictly true. Some straw on which he slept, a square block of wood, a low, three-legged stool, and an old tea-caddy, are the complete inventory of the articles of a room, the occupier of which, with only himself and his wife to maintain, was wealthier than many in the station of gentlemen. He had frequently excited lively compassion in benevolent individuals, who supposing that he was struggling for very existence, furnished him with a variety of household goods, which were regularly pawned before a week was out, and afforded to the superficial observer fresh evidence of the extremity of his distress. The cause of all this is quickly told: the wife was to be seen going to and fro several times a-day with a cream jug of gin, and to gratify this appetite, they had voluntarily reduced themselves to the condition of savages. I could add numerous instances of a similar kind. Indeed, were a stranger to go through the town, and judge only from the appearance of things, I am convinced that he would select his examples of greatest privation not from the really poor, but from men who were in the receipt of more then 30s. a-week. Charity, which

when promoted by pure motives, always blesses him that gives, does not always bless him that takes . . .

Ragged Schools

Homeless waifs, and pauper children whose contacts with their families were extremely tenuous, were to be seen in large numbers in any of the country's big cities during the nineteenth century. Ragged schools were established to rescue these children from the consequences of their condition. In MEMOIR OF THOMAS GUTHRIE, DD *(1875), D. K. and C. J. Guthrie wrote of the origins and intentions of the schools.*

Year after year, a fresh crop of miserable young creatures was suffered to grow up, for whom no man seemed to care. Passing through the various stages of juvenile delinquency, they developed ere long into hardened criminals, and so, continuously, the process went on; nor was it until the children of the streets had committed crime, and found themselves within the grim walls of a cell, that the country thought of providing them with clothing, or food either for mind or body. To arrest a main stream of sin and sorrow at its very fountain head—to lay hold of those who are 'ready to perish' ere they have got hopelessly beyond our reach—is an endeavour as wise and patriotic as it is Christian; and few men nowadays will dispute the need or value of Ragged Schools.

Let it be understood that a Ragged School—in the sense of the term used by Dr Guthrie—implies a school where, along with education both sacred and secular, food, clothing, and industrial training are gratuitously supplied. The honour of having devised these admirable institutions belongs to Sheriff Watson, who in 1841 opened in Aberdeen the first

40 *Ragged Schools sometimes found work for their pupils. The boy in the picture below was licensed as a shoe-black*

41 *A drawing (c1870) showing Dr Barnado searching for waifs and strays in London. His charitable work began in Ragged Schools, but he extended his activities by founding the Home for Destitute Boys in Stepney— the first of the Dr Barnado's Homes*

Ragged (or, to use his term) Industrial Feeding School.

The Charity Organisation Society
The Central Relief Society in Liverpool (founded 1863) and the Charity Organisation Society in London (founded 1870) were pioneer groups which united various charities and introduced a more discriminate approach to the problem of relieving poverty. P. F.

69

Ashcrott, a German political economist, described the COS in THE ENGLISH POOR LAW SYSTEM (1886).

The organisation takes place in the following fashion. The district committees of the society act for areas corresponding with the poor law unions and parishes of the metropolis. There are at present 40 district committees. It is desired, whenever possible, to obtain the election of members of the district committees as guardians, in order to establish relations with the administration of poor relief . . .

The co-operation of the Charity Organisation Society with the guardians is, to a large extent, effected through the relieving officers. The relieving officer is asked to inform the district committee of all cases which appear suitable for private charity; on the other hand, the relieving officer is made acquainted with each case applying to the district committee. In this way it is possible to prevent relief from being given simultaneously to one and the same person, both from the poor law and from private charity . . .

Searching enquiries, by which full details are obtained as to the cause of poverty, are absolutely necessary, in order to distinguish charitable from poor law cases, and to settle the proper means of relief to the former. Such enquiries are for the most part made by paid officers of the society.

Model Village

The Cadbury family ran a large chocolate industry, but they were also Quakers with a social conscience. In addition to charitable intentions, George Cadbury had the dedication and ability to undertake practical measures to help his workers, and Bournville became a model for town planners. The following description is from THE LIFE OF GEORGE CADBURY *by A. G. Gardiner (1923).*

. . . he began by purchasing 120 acres of land in the neighbourhood of the works, an area which gradually increased to 842 acres including the property of the firm. He had long seen that the monopoly of the land

was the source of bad housing conditions, and he had adopted the axiom of the land reformers, that land, as a necessary of life, should be used not to create wealth for individuals but to serve the interests of the community . . . His aim was to solve the whole problem of housing and town-planning, and while he employed the most competent professional advice and consulted anyone whose experience was valuable, he made it his chief task to supervise the experiment and control the main lines of its development. He had clear and decisive views on all points. He planned the roads, the grouping of the trees, the elevations of the houses, the width of the pavements, the amount of garden space, the proportion of land allocated to park and playgrounds, and so on . . . He began by building 143 houses which he sold at cost price, on a lease of 999 years for the ground on which they stood. His idea was that the tenure should be as near freehold as possible; but the condition of the lease made it impossible that the gardens should be destroyed or built over. Half the purchase cost was advanced at the low rate of $2\frac{1}{2}$ per cent interest, and loans in excess of this half paid interest at the rate of 3 per cent.

Co-operation with Public Authorities

The depressed areas created by the collapse of established industries during the 1930s presented a problem of such magnitude that a combined operation was mounted, involving various agencies engaged in relief of the poor—the government, a supervisory body set up by the government, a multi-millionaire's trust fund, and a charitable organisation. The ANNUAL REGISTER *of 1935 reported the proposal. Unfortunately the aims were not realised.*

. . . [There were] certain agricultural schemes under the supervision of a private body known as the Land Settlement Association. This body had been formed in 1934 at the request of the Minister of Agriculture to test the feasibility of the economic

42 *'The Silken Lady' giving away food and drink during the hungry 30s. She and her fashionable friends had found a constructive amusement*

settlement of unemployed men on the land. At the end of the year the Commissioner for the Special Areas, Mr Malcolm Stewart, had presented it with an estate of 25,000 acres at Patton in Bedfordshire, and in addition had offered to pay one-third of the cost of settlement where men were transferred from his areas. The Government also had offered to contribute £75,000 a year for three years on a pound for pound basis of subscriptions received by the Association, and the Carnegie Trust had offered to contribute £150,000, spread over five years. The Association considered that it required £1,000,000 for carrying out the experiments on a proper scale, and for the remainder of this sum it was now appealing to the public.

CHAPTER FIVE

HELP FOR THE LABOURING POOR

When people became destitute their needs were obvious, and government help was easily justified. Less obvious, and for a long time considered to be outside the scope of government, was the need for action to protect the labouring poor from the adverse effects of the economic system. Such action, aimed at providing security and fair treatment for underprivileged workers, consisted of placing restraints on employers and traders whose practices were causing the poor to suffer; and as might be expected these people resisted any legislation which affected their interests.

*The governments of James I and Charles I made a limited contribution towards helping the labouring poor by introducing measures to stop evictions, control food supplies, and regulate prices. But the following two hundred years witnessed the success of landlords, employers, suppliers, and the advocates of laissez-faire in ensuring that measures affecting their interests were generally in abeyance. Not until the 1830s did the legislators take a fresh initiative. From this time on-*wards *they took positive steps to counter exploitation, improve conditions of service, provide amenities, and regularise income. The justice of securing protection for the labouring poor was increasingly acknowledged, and the responsibility of the legislators in this field was accepted.*

Regulations Concerning Corn

The badgers, engrossers, and forestallers of the seventeenth century were the middlemen (regrators) who exploited the corn markets. Badgers bought up corn in one area to sell in another, while engrossers and forestallers bought corn privately (sometimes while it was still growing) to sell later when prices were higher. Their activities, and those of middlemen of later centuries, were circumscribed in times of shortage by price regulation—the assize of bread and ale—and by limiting their quotas.

About limiting of Badgers to a certaine quantity in buying of Corne

The last of November 1630 . . . First, wee require you to take very carefull order that no Badger be permitted either to buy anie graine in anie Market, save onely such a quantitie as shall be limitted by you or other Justices of the Peace, or to give anie extraordinarie or great price by the Bushell or quarter but such as may be moderate and after the rate of six shillings eight pence or seaven shillings the Bushell for Wheat and proporcionally for other graine, which is conceived upon the conference that hath beene had with sundry Farmers and Corn-masters to be an indifferent rate and price betweene the buyer and seller. Secondly, you are to take lyke Order that no Badger buy above ten quarters of all maner of graine in anie one Market.

[ACTS OF THE PRIVY COUNCIL OF ENGLAND (1664)]

Measures of Corn and Bread

1 quarter	=2 coombs	The peck loaf=17lb 6oz
1 coomb	=4 bushels	The quartern loaf=
1 bushel	=4 pecks	4lb 5oz 8dr
1 peck	=2 gallons	1 stone=14lb

A report from the Sheriff of Norfolk showed how the Justices of the Peace took steps to keep the price of corn down.

March 3 1631. Francis Mayes, Sheriff of Norfolk, to the Council. Reports the contents of three returns received from Justices of various divisions of that county respecting the state of the corn markets and the price of corn. Among the measures adopted for diminishing the consumption of grain, one was not to license ale houses but to such as would enter into a recognizance not to sell a less quantity than two full 'thurdendeles' of beer, according to his Majesty's standard, for a penny. Throughout the county the price of corn was deemed excessive; in one division the authorities laid in a store, and sold the same to the poor, viz. rye at 3s. 4d. the bushel, barley at 2s. 6d., buck at 20d.

[CALENDAR OF STATE PAPERS, DOMESTIC SERIES, 1629-31]

It was customary for magistrates to publish the controlled price of bread in local newspapers. The assize below is taken from the LEICESTER JOURNAL *of 31 January 1817.*

The Assize of Bread for the Hundred of GARTREE, in the county of Leicester,
The Weight and Price of

	lb	oz	dr	£	s	d
The Peck Loaf wheaten	17	6	0	0	5	4
Half Peck Loaf wheaten	8	11	0	0	2	8
Quartern Loaf wheaten	4	5	8	0	1	4
Half Quartern Loaf wheaten	2	2	12	0	0	8
The Peck Loaf household	17	6	0	0	5	0
Half Peck Loaf household	8	11	0	0	2	6
Quartern Loaf household	4	5	8	0	1	3
Half Quartern Loaf ditto	2	2	12	0	0	7½

Set by us Two of his Majesty's Justices of the Peace in and for the said Hundred, the 28th day of January 1817, and to continue in force for seven days from Monday next.

F. GRIFFIN
JAS. ORD.

The Problem of Inadequate Wages

When labour was in short supply, magistracies were empowered to fix maximum wages to protect the employer, but no one had any success with minimum wage Bills until the early twentieth century. Despite the advocacy of the great parliamentarian Fox, part of whose speech is given below, Whitbread's Minimum Wage Bill of 1795 was defeated.

The act of Elizabeth, as his hon. friend had truly stated, empowered the justices to fix the highest price of labour, but it gave them no power to fix the lowest. It secured the master from a risk that could but seldom occur, of being charged exorbitantly for the quantity of service; but it did not authorise the magistrate to protect the poor from the injustice of a griping and avaricious employer, who might be disposed to take advantage of their necessities, and under-value the rate of their service. If the price of labour was adequate to the support of the poor at ordinary times, though not equal to the accidental high price of provisions at the present moment, it might be contended that there was less necessity for any new legislative regulation. But, taking the average price of labour for some years past, including that period during which the scarcity had operated, no man could deny that the price of labour was greatly disproportionate to the rate of provisions.

[PARLIAMENTARY HISTORY, Vol 33]

Agricultural crisis, aggravated by war, induced the Berkshire magistrates in 1795 to introduce their famous system of subsidising wages. This failed in its objective, because the farmers' reaction was to lower wages, which caused the poor rates to shoot up. The resolution below is taken from the report of the Speenhamland meeting which appeared in the READING MERCURY *on 11 May 1795.*

Resolved,

When the Gallon Loaf of Second Flour, weighing 8lb. 11oz. shall cost 1s.

Then every poor and industrious man shall have for his own support 3s. weekly, either produced by his own or his family's labour, or an allowance from the poor rates, and for the support of his wife and every other of his family, 1s. 6d.

When the Gallon Loaf shall cost 1s. 4d.

Then every poor and industrious man shall have 4s. weekly for his own, and 1s. and 10d. for the support of every other of his family.

And so in proportion, as the price of bread rise or falls (that is to say) 3d. to the man, and 1d. to every other of the family, on every 1d. which the loaf rise above 1s.

Reaction Against Drunkenness

One of the few original legislative contributions of

43 *A tavern scene in the early nineteenth century, illustrating the various evils associated with strong drink*

the eighteenth century was the attempt to save the urban poor from their own bad habits. An example of this attempt was the GIN ACT *of 1751.*

Whereas the immoderate drinking of distilled spirituous liquors by persons of the meanest sort, hath of late years increased, to the great detriment of the health and morals of the common people; and the same hath in great measure been owing to the number of persons who have obtained licences to retail the same, under pretence of being distillers, and of those who have presumed to retail the same without licence . . . contrary to the good and wholesome laws heretofore made for preventing thereof: and whereas your Majesty's dutiful and loyal subjects the commons of Great Britain in parliament assembled, ever attentive to the preservation and health of your Majesty's subjects, have taken this great evil into our serious consideration, and proposed such laws and provisions as appear to us likely to put a stop to the same . . .

VIII And for the further restriction of such licences, and the granting thereof, be it enacted by the authority aforesaid, That no licence for the selling by retail of spirituous liquors shall be granted within the limits of the head office of excise in *London*, but to such as shall occupy a tenement or tenements of the yearly value of ten pounds or upwards, and for which they shall accordingly be rated and pay in the parish rates; nor to any person in any other part of the kingdom, where there are rates to church and poor, but to such as shall be possessed and pay to the church and poor in the several parishes and places in which they shall be respectively licensed . . .

XIII And be it further enacted by the authority aforesaid, That no licence shall be granted for the retailing of spirituous liquors within any gaol, prison, house of correction, workhouse, or house of entertainment for any parish poor . . .

The nineteenth century saw the campaign against drinking extended to beer, and despite the brewers'

formidable lobbying the Licensing Act of 1872 was passed, restricting hours of opening as well as reducing the number of public houses. The following extract from the COAL MINES REGULATION ACT (1842) *illustrates an early stage in the campaign.*

And whereas the practice of paying wages to workmen at public houses is found to be highly injurious to the best interests of the working classes; be it therefore enacted, that from and after the expiration of three months from the passing of this act no proprietor or worker of any mine or colliery, or other person, shall pay or cause to be paid any wages . . . at or within any tavern, public house, beer shop, or other house of entertainment.

Henry Mayhew used his magazine LONDON LABOUR AND THE LONDON POOR (*the issue of 28 October 1851*) *to inveigh against drunkenness among the working classes.*

The misfortune is, that many operatives positively look upon beer as necessary for the performance of hard labour; whereas it is a physiological fact, that the stimulus derived from the imbibition of fermented liquors is followed by a corresponding amount of depression, so that just as much as a man gains in energy at one time does he lose at another. The poor man's energy is his sole patrimony; so that to spend money on stimulating beverages is not only to waste his hard earnings upon a brutal propensity, but to deprive himself of the power of getting more. This want of energy is a marked feature in every drunkard's character; the unshorn beard, the untidy home, the deferred work, are all proofs that the main evil of drink to working men lies in the destruction of those energies from which they derive their substance . . .

Protection for Workers in Industry

New problems created by the Industrial Revolution led governments to inquire into working conditions, and after some timid legislation at the beginning of the nineteenth century they interfered more positively in spheres which they had previously regarded as being outside their compass.

Payment in kind ('truck') or in tokens which could only be spent at the factory shop ('tommy shop') had become notorious abuses. In both cases the labourer received much less than the face value of his wages, as goods were priced artificially high. THE TRUCK ACT

44 *Token issued by John Pinkerton to the workmen on the Basingstoke Canal*

OF *1831, cited below, was designed to stop all this, but as Disraeli pointed out in* Sybil, *by paying wages irregularly the overseer could run very profitable 'tommy shops' by selling goods on account.*

In contracts for the hiring of artificers, wages must be made payable in the current coin of the realm. In all contracts hereafter to be made for the hiring of any artificer in any of the trades hereinafter enumerated or for the performance by any artificer of any labour in any of the said trades, the wages of such artificer shall be made payable in the current coin of this realm only, and not otherwise; and if in any such contract the whole or any part of such wages shall be made payable in any manner other than in the current coin aforesaid, such contract shall be and is hereby declared illegal, null, and void.

The REPORT OF THE GOVERNMENT COMMISSION ON MINES (1842) *shocked the country, and the subsequent Act banned women and children from the coal face.*

The statements of all classes of witnesses concur in showing that the labour to which these female workers are subjected is unexampled in severity and most revolting in its nature, but more especially the statements of the girls and young women themselves. Helen Reid, sixteen years old, coal-bearer: 'I have wrought five years in the mines in this part; my employment is carrying coal. Am frequently worked from four in the morning until six at night. I work night-work week about. I then go down at two in the day, and come up at four and six in the morning. I can carry two cwt. on my back. I do not like the work. Two years since the pit closed upon 13 of us, and we were two days without food or light; for nearly one day we were up to our chins in water. At last we got to an old shaft, to which we picked our way, and were heard by people watching above. Two months ago I was filling the tubs at the pit bottom, when the gig clicked too early, and the hook caught me by my pit-clothes—the people did not hear my shrieks—my hand had fast grappled the chain, and the great height of the shaft caused me to lose my courage and I swooned. The banksman could scarcely remove my hand—the deadly grasp saved my life.'

The Sub-Commissioner represents this labour as 'a cruel slaving revolting to humanity'; yet he found engaged in this labour a child, a beautiful girl, only six years old, whose age he ascertained, carrying in the pit $\frac{1}{2}$ cwt. of coals, and regularly making with this load fourteen long and toilsome journeys a day. Ellison Jack, a girl eleven years old, coal-bearer: 'I have been working below three years on my father's account; he takes me down at two in the morning, and I come up at one or two next afternoon. I go to bed at six at night to be ready for work next morning; the part of the pit I bear in, the seams are much on the edge. I have to bear my burthen up four traps, or ladders, before I get to the main road which leads to the pit bottom. My task is four to five tubs; each tub holding $4\frac{1}{4}$ cwt. I fill five tubs in 20 journeys. I

45 *'Capital and Labour'. A Punch cartoon of 1843, emphasising the great gulf between rich and poor*

have had the strap when I did not do my bidding. I am very glad when my task is wrought as it sore fatigues.'

Fielden's TEN HOURS' ACT (1847)—*quoted below— introduced the ten-hour working day for women and children, but not until 1874 was the ten-hour day for men achieved.*

Whereas an Act was passed in the Fourth Year of the Reign of His late Majesty, intituled *An Act to regulate the labour of Children and young Persons in the Mills and Factories of the United Kingdom;* and

another Act was passed in the Session of Parliament held in the Seventh and Eighth Years of the Reign of Her present Majesty, intituled *An Act to amend the Laws relating to Labour in Factories;* and by the said first mentioned Act it was provided that no Person under the Age of Eighteen Years should be employed in any such Mill or Factory as in the said Act is mentioned . . . more than Twelve Hours in any One Day, nor more than Sixty-nine Hours in any One Week, except as thereinafter is provided; and by the said last mentioned Act it was provided, that no Female above the Age of Eighteen Years should be employed in any Factory as defined by the said Act, save for the same Time and in the same Manner as young Persons (by the said Act defined to be Persons of the Age of Thirteen Years and under the Age of Eighteen Years) might be employed in Factories . . . be it enacted that from the First Day of May One thousand eight hundred and forty-eight no Person under the Age of Eighteen Years shall be employed in any such Mill or Factory, in such Description of Work as in the said first-mentioned Act is specified, for more than Ten Hours in any One Day . . .

III. And be it enacted, That the Restrictions respectively by this Act imposed as regards the working of Persons under the Age of Eighteen Years shall extend to Females above the Age of Eighteen Years.

Health Reform

Disraeli's Tory government of 1874-80 produced a number of health reforms, and one of them, the Artisans' Dwellings Act, had a deep social significance; for the first time public money was to be spent on a particular section of the community—the labouring class. The account below is from the ANNUAL REGISTER *of 1875.*

The first Bill of the Session, in point of time, was that introduced by Mr. Cross, the Home Secretary, on February the 8th, to facilitate the Improvement of Dwellings for the Working Classes in towns. He started from the position that the consideration of the public health should form the exclusive object to be kept in view in any legislation dealing with this question. It was not, he said at the outset of his speech, the business of a Government to provide any class of citizens with any of the necessaries of life, and good and habitable dwellings are one of the chief necessaries of life. Nor was it expedient for a Government to encourage large bodies of persons to provide the working classes with habitations at greatly lower rents than the market value paid elsewhere. But, on the other hand, it is not only wise and expedient, but the imperative duty of a Government,

to take care that the houses which this or any other class do in fact occupy should not become centres of disease and of the conditions which propagate the disease. He brought forward many facts to prove the urgency of the case. In Liverpool there are courts, containing more than 2,000 people, in which there have been more people sick in five years than the whole population; and there is not one house in which there has not been a death annually. The average death-rate of the whole country is a little over 22 per 1,000; but in Manchester there is a district in which the rate is now 67 per 1,000 . . .

. . . The measure, however, passed with little alteration, though some critics objected to the limitation of its provisions to towns of 25,000 inhabitants. Under its provisions corporations may, on the report of their medical officers, acquire buildings by compulsory purchase for the purpose of improvement. They may either build or let the land for building in accordance with schemes which they are to prepare with special regard to the accommodation of the working classes.

Action Against 'Sweat Shops'

By the end of the nineteenth century, trade unions were negotiating the wages of their members, but there were still the 'sweat shops' to be considered. The Trade Boards Act (1909) finally imposed a minimum-wage structure, after such exhibitions as that described by F. A. Iremonger in WILLIAM TEMPLE, ARCHBISHOP OF CANTERBURY (1948) *had publicised the situation.*

[In 1907] a Sweated Industries Exhibition was held at Oxford. Here Temple saw the results of a *laissez-faire* industrial system: match-boxes made at the rate of 2d. a gross, the worker having to find paste, hemp (for tying up), and firing to dry wet boxes, spending 2 hours a day in fetching and returning her work, and receiving 8s. a week for 10 hours' toil a day; trousers which were basted, machined, finished, and pressed at a net wage of 6s. a week for 12 hours'

80

hard daily work; artificial flowers for the making of which the worker provided her own paste, and earned an average of 10s. a week for a 14-hour day: stall after stall decked with the produce of free enterprise, including one devoted to the wages and hours that prevailed in the industry of 'Biblefolding'.

National Insurance and National Assistance

Health insurance for all manual workers and unemployment insurance for men working in certain industries were introduced by Lloyd George, as Chancellor of the Exchequer, in 1911. In both cases government and employer contributed, as well as the workman. This far-reaching reform was inspired by Germany's example.

An Act to provide for Insurance against Loss of Health and Cure of Sickness and for Insurance against Unemployment, and for purposes incidental thereto . . .

8(1) Subject to the provisions of this Act, the benefits conferred by this part of this Act upon insured persons are—

a) Medical treatment and attendance, including the provision of proper and sufficient medicines, and such medical surgical appliances as may be prescribed by regulations to be made by the Insurance Commissioners . . .

c) Periodical payments whilst rendered incapable of work by some specific disease or by bodily or mental disablement . . . continuing for a period not exceeding twenty-six weeks . . .

85(1) The sums required for the payment of unemployment benefit under this Act shall be derived

46 *Children spinning yarn. The Factory Act of 1833 forbade the employment of children as young as this*

partly from contributions by workmen in the insured trades and partly from contributions by employers of such workmen and partly from moneys provided by Parliament . . .

(6) A contribution shall be made in each year out of moneys provided by Parliament equal to one-third of the total contributions received from employers and workmen during that year . . .

[NATIONAL INSURANCE ACT, 1911]

The UNEMPLOYMENT ASSISTANCE ACT *of 1934 created the National Assistance Board which was independent of local control and party politics—a major step forward. The Board's operations, however, aroused great resentment, for its scales of relief were low, and its local investigators applied the invidious 'needs test' harshly.*

35 (2) The functions of the Board shall be the assistance of persons . . . who are in need of work and the promotion of their welfare and, in particular, the making of provision for the improvement and re-establishment of such persons with a view to their being in all respects fit for entry into or return to regular employment, and the grant and issue to such persons of unemployment allowances . . .

(3) For the purpose of securing the advice and assistance of persons having local knowledge and experience in matters affecting the functions of the Board under this part of the Act, the Board shall arrange for the establishment of advisory committees throughout Great Britain to act for such areas as the Board think fit . . .

38 (2) The amount of any allowance to be granted . . . to an applicant shall be determined by reference to his needs, including the needs of any members of the household of which he is a member who are dependent on or ordinarily supported by him . . .

CHAPTER SIX

HELP FOR THE DESTITUTE POOR

From the time of the Elizabethan Poor Law the government assumed responsibility for relieving those who were destitute, and numerous measures were introduced to this end, but the poor were regarded with the utmost suspicion. Acts of Parliament warned against indulgent treatment of the 'idle poor'; social commentators suggested that much poverty was the result of defects of character; and the payers of poor rates protested that their money was often used to support undeserving cases. Against this background the Justices of the Peace, who were responsible for the administration of laws in their locality, were often inclined to reject the idea that there could be virtuous poor, and saw the relief of poverty as a corrective process rather than as a mission of charity. Out of such attitudes grew the infamous Poor Law Amendment Act of 1834. The effects of this Act were softened later by measures aimed at saving the poor from destitution, and by the sympathetic approach adopted by some of the boards of guardians, but even in the twentieth century we

find examples of reaction against heavy costs resulting in inadequate provision for those in genuine need.

The First Poor Laws

The Elizabethan Poor Laws of 1598 and 1601 were inspired by the need to cope with a problem which had got completely out of hand.

Be it enacted by the authoritie of this present Parliament, that the Churchwardens of every Parish, and foure, three or two substantiall housholders there, as shall be thought meete, having respect to the proportion and greatnesse of the same Parish and Parishes, to be nominated yeerely in Easter weeke, or within one Moneth after Easter, under the hand and seale of two or more Justices of the Peace in the same Countie, whereof one to be of the Quorum, dwelling in or near the same Parish or division, where the same Parish doth lye, shall bee called Overseers of the poore of the same Parish. And they, or the greater part of them shall take order from time to time, by, and with

the consent of two or more such Justices of peace, as is aforesaid, for setting to worke of the children of all such, whose parents shall not by the said Church-wardens and Overseers, or the greater part of them, be thought able to keepe and maintain their children. And also for setting to worke all such persons maried, or unmaried, having no meanes to maintaine them, use no ordinarie and daily trade of life to get their living by, and also to raise weekely, or otherwise (by taxation of every Inhabitant, Parson, Vicar, and other, and of every occupier of landes, houses, tythes impropriate, or propriations of tythes, colemines, or saleable underwoods in the said Parish, in such competent summe and summes of money, as they shall thinke fit) a convenient Stocke of Flaxe, Hempe, Wooll, Threed, Iron, and other necessarie ware and stuffe to set the poore on worke, and also competent summes of money, for, and towardes the necessarie relief of the lame, impotent, old, blinde, and such other among them being poore, and not able to worke, and also for the putting out of such chidren to be apprentices, to be gathered out of the same Parish, according to the abilitie of the same Parish, and to doe, and execute all other things, as well for the disposing of the said stocke, as otherwise concerning the premisses, as to them shall seeme convenient . . .
[AN ACT FOR THE RELIEF OF THE POORE, 1601]

Supervision of Poor Relief

It was soon obvious that JPs were neglecting their duties under the Act of 1601, and after bad harvests in 1629 and 1630 Charles I's council was at pains to ensure that the Poor Law's provisions were observed. Later governments did not follow this example.

. . . appointing them to be Commissioners for inquiring into the execution of the laws which anyway concerns the relief of the poor, the binding out of apprentices, the setting to work poor people, the compelling the lazy to work, the maintenance of houses of correction, payment for relief of soldiers and mariners, punishment of rogues and vagabonds, repressing drunkenness, keeping watch and ward, and how other public services for God, the King, and the Commonwealth, are put in practice and executed.
[CALENDAR OF STATE PAPERS DOMESTIC, 1629-31]

A chain of responsibility was carefully established to guard against laxity among the JPs.

Order of the Lords Commissioners under the Commission of the 5th Jan for inquiring into the execution of the laws for the relief of the poor, whereby the whole kingdom was partitioned out among the Commissioners, to the end that the Justices of the Peace should give an account monthly to the Sheriffs, and the Sheriffs send up those accounts to the Judges of the several circuits, who were every term to give them to the Lords Commissioners.
[CALENDER OF STATE PAPERS DOMESTIC, 1631-33]

The Commonwealth Parliament, which governed for a short time after Charles I's execution in 1649, concerned itself with ridding London of its destitute poor by adopting punitive measures.

. . . And it is further enacted by the authority aforesaid; That it is, and shall bee lawfull, to, and for the said President and Governours of the said Corporation, for the time being, or any two of them, any two of them, to apprehend, or cause to bee apprehended, any Rogues, Vagrants, Sturdy Beggers, idle and disorderly persons within the said City, and Liberties, and to cause them to bee set and kept to work; And such of them as by any former Statute, are declared to bee Rogues, to bee duly punished by putting in the Stocks, or whipping, as they shall find cause; And also have power to dispose of them to their places of birth, or last abode, as the case, according to the Laws and Statutes in that case provided shall require; And also that it shall bee lawfull for the said President, and Governours, or any two of them, to apprehnd, or cause to bee apprehended, and kept at work. All such other Poore persons, and Bastard children, and other

47, 48 *Children of the poor at the end of the seventeenth century (from Tempest's* Cryes of London, *1711).*
(Left) Sellers of laces (right) Apprentice sweep

Poore children able to work, and inhabiting within the said City and Liberties, who are chargeable to any Parish, or have not sufficient to maintaine themselves; and in case of their refusall so to work; That then it shall and may bee lawfull, to and for the said President, and Governours, or any seven of them to punish, or cause to bee punished as Vagrants, such persons so refusing to work; . . .

[AN ACT . . . FOR THE RELIEF, AND IMPLOYMENT OF THE POOR, AND THE PUNISHING OF VAGRANTS AND OTHER DISORDERLY PERSONS WITHIN THE CITY OF LONDON, AND LIBERTIES THEREOF, 1649]

Workhouses and Outdoor Relief

Gregory King, in the state and condition of England 1696, *recorded that almshouses and endowed hospitals*

in *England were catering for 13,400 paupers, and the idea of setting up workhouses was already gaining support. Daniel Defoe, addressing Parliament in* GIVING ALMS NO CHARITY (1704), *echoed the prejudices which were the bane of poor law enforcement.*

Work-houses, Corporations, Parish-stocks, and the like, to set them to Work, as they are Pernicious to Trade, Injurious and Impoverishing to those already employ'd so they are needless, and will come short of the end proposed.

The Poverty and Exigence of the Poor in *England* is plainly deriv'd from one of these two particular Causes,

Casualty or Crime.

By Casualty, I mean Sickness of Families, loss of Limbs or Sight, and any, either Natural or Accidental Impotence as to Labour.

These as Infirmities mearly Providential are not at all concern'd in this Debate; ever were, will, and ought to be the Charge and Care of the Respective Parishes where such unhappy People chance to live, nor is there any want of new Laws to make Provision for them, our Ancestors having been always careful to do it.

The Crimes of our People, and from whence their Poverty derives, as the visible and direct Fountains are,

1. Luxury
2. Sloath
3. Pride

. . . the profuse Extravagant Humour of our poor People in eating and drinking, keeps them low, causes their Children to be left naked and starving, to the care of the Parishes, whenever either Sickness or Disaster befalls the Parent . . . This is the Ruine of our Poor, the Wife *mourns*, the Children *starves*, the Husband *has Work before him*, but lies at the Ale-house, or otherwise *idles away* his time, and won't Work.

'Tis the Men that *won't work*, not the Men that

can get no work, which makes the numbers of our Poor; all the Workhouse in England, all the Overseers setting up Stocks and Manufactures won't reach this Case; and I humbly presume to say, if these two Articles are remov'd, there will be no need of the other.

W. Hutton, who wrote AN HISTORY OF BIRMINGHAM *in 1783, was proud of the town's workhouse but was constrained to note characteristics of the poor law which entailed much suffering. He referred to the practice of binding out paupers (men and children) to an apprenticeship which approached slavery, and to the Act of Settlement (1662) which insisted that a pauper could only receive relief from his native parish.*

Though the poor were nursed by parochial law,

49 *Defoe was more famous for his novels, but much of his writing took the form of reactionary social comment (portrait from* Jure Divino, *1706)*

yet workhouses did not become general 'till 1730: that of Birmingham was erected in 1733, at the expence of £1173 3s 5d. and which, the stranger would rather suppose, was the residence of a gentleman, than that of four hundred paupers. The left wing, called the infirmary, was added in 1766, at the charge of £400 and the right, a place for labour, in 1779, at the expence of £700 more . . . Whether the mode of distributing the bounty of the community, is agreeable to the intentions of legislature, or the ideas of humanity, is a doubt. For in some parishes the unfortunate paupers have the additional misery of being sold to a mercenary wretch to starve upon 12d a head. It is a matter of surprise that the magistrate should wink at this cruelty; but it is a matter of pleasure, that no accusation comes within the verge of my historical remarks, for the wretched of Birmingham are not made more so by ill treatment, but meet with a kindness acceptable to distress . . . We cannot be conversant in parochial business, without observing a littleness predominant in most parishes, by using every finesse to relieve themselves of paupers, and throwing them upon others. Thus the oppressed, like the child between two fathers, is supported by neither.

There is also an enormity, which, though agreeable to law, can never be justified by the rules of equity— That a man should spend the principal part of his life in a parish, add wealth to it by his labour, form connexions in it, bring up a family which shall all belong to it, but having never gained a settlement himself, shall, in old age, be removed by an order, to perish among strangers.

For the poet George Crabbe the main characteristic of the workhouses was their inhumanity. He wrote THE VILLAGE *in 1783.*

Their's is yon House that holds the Parish Poor,
Whose walls of mud scarce bear the broken door;
There, where the putrid vapours flagging, play,
and the dull wheel hums doleful through the day;—

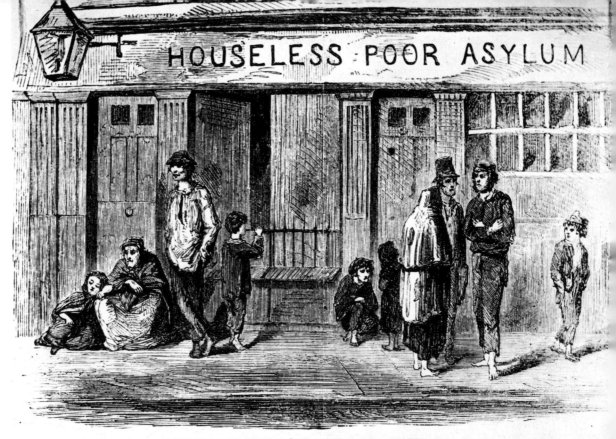

ASYLUM FOR THE HOUSELESS POOR, CRIPPLEGATE.

50 *One of the workhouses set up in the eighteenth century*

There Children dwell who know no Parents' care;
Parents, who know no Children's love, dwell there;
Heart-broken Matrons on their joyless bed,
Forsaken Wives and Mothers never wed;
Dejected widows with unheeded tears,
and crippled Age with more than childhood-fears;
The Lame, the Blind, and, far the happiest they!
The moping Idiot and the Madman gay.
Here too the Sick their final doom receive,
Here brought amid the scenes of grief, to grieve;
Where the loud groans from some sad chamber flow,
Mixt with the clamours of the crowd below;
. . . .
Anon, a Figure enters, quaintly neat,
All pride and business, bustle and conceit;
With looks unalter'd by these scenes of woe,
With speed that, entering, speaks his haste to go;
He bids the gazing throng around him fly,

And carries Fate and Physic in his eye;
A potent Quack, long vers'd in human ills,
Who first insults the victim whom he kills;
Whose murd'rous hand a drowsy Bench protect,
And whose most tender mercy is neglect.
Paid by the Parish for attendance here,
He wears contempt upon his sapient sneer;
In haste he seeks the bed where Misery lies,
Impatience mark'd in his averted eyes;
And, some habitual queries hurried o'er,
Without reply, he rushes on the door;
His drooping Patient, long inur'd to pain,
And long unheeded, knows remonstrance vain;
He ceases now the feeble help to crave
Of Man; and silent sinks into the grave.

   In AN ESSAY ON THE PRINCIPLE OF POPULATION (1798), *Thomas Malthus startled the world with his forecasts of increases in population (which, in the event, were very conservative). He considered that the operation of the poor law added to the problem.*

The poor-laws of England tend to depress the general condition of the poor in these two ways. Their first obvious tendency is to increase population without increasing the food for its support. A poor man may marry with little or no prospect of being able to support a family in independence. They may be said therefore in some measure to create the poor which they maintain; and as the provisions of the country must, in consequence of the increased population, be distributed to every man in smaller proportions, it is evident that the labour of those who are not supported by parish assistance, will purchase a smaller quantity of provisions than before, and consequently, more of them must be driven to ask for support.

Secondly, the quantity of provisions consumed in workhouses upon a part of the society, that cannot in general be considered as the most valuable part, diminishes the shares that would otherwise belong to more industrious, and more worthy members; and thus in the same manner forces more to become dependent. If the poor in the workhouses were to live better than they now do, this new distribution of the money of the society would tend more conspicuously to depress the condition of those out of the workhouses, by occasioning a rise in the price of provisions.

Fortunately for England, a spirit of independence still remains among the peasantry. The poor-laws are strongly calculated to eradicate this spirit. They have

51 'A Workhouse Dinner' by Jas Grant (1840)

succeeded in part, but had they succeeded as completely as might have been expected, their pernicious tendency would not have been as long concealed.

Joseph Lowe was less emotional than Crabbe, but still found the workhouses falling far short of their objectives. It is interesting to compare his estimate of workhouse capacity in 1882 (when THE PRESENT STATE OF ENGLAND *was published) with the estimate of King over a century before.*

The work-house plan, originally adopted above a century ago, received a great extension from an act passed in 1782, commonly called Gilbert's Act, from the name of the member of parliament by whom it was framed. This act, aiming to combine the advantages of an assemblage of a number of poor on one spot, of a minute division of labour, and a joint management of disburse, empowered all magistrates to consider any large work-house as a common receptacle for the poor throughout a diameter of twenty miles. Sound as these reasons apparently were, the plan has as yet been by no means successful: proper care has seldom been taken to separate the inmates of the work-houses according to their age or their habits; nor has the division of employment been at all carried to the necessary length. Their earnings have consequently been insignificant, and the charge to the parish amounts, in general, to £9, £10, or even £12 per head, while half the sum would suffice, if paid to the poor at their own habitations. It is thus in some measure fortunate that the limited extent of our work-houses hardly admits above 100,000 individuals.

The aim of the Poor Law Amendment Act of 1834 was to lower the poor rate and discourage idleness. Tales of workhouse conditions following this Act are well known—guardians of the poor zealously pursued the recommendations that the able-bodied pauper should be less comfortable than the meanest labourer, but hardly any poor law unions set up separate workhouses for the different classes of poor.

The chief specific measures which we recommend are:—

First, that except as to medical attendance, and subject to the exception respecting apprenticeship hereinafter stated, all relief whatever to able-bodied persons or to their families, otherwise than in well-regulated workhouses (i.e., places where they may be set to work according to the spirit and intention of the 43rd of Elizabeth), shall be declared unlawful, and shall cease, in manner and at periods hereafter specified; and that all relief afforded in respect of children under the age of 16, shall be considered as afforded to their parents. . . .

. . . At least four classes are necessary:—(1) The aged and really impotent; (2) The children; (3) The able-bodied females; (4) The able-bodies males. Of whom we trust that the two latter will be the least numerous classes. It appears to us that both the requisite classification and the requisite superintendence may be better obtained in separate buildings than under a single roof. . . .

[REPORT FROM THE COMMISSION ON THE POOR LAWS, 1834]

A Return to Out-relief

The widespread hostility to the workhouse system enforced by the Act of 1834 led to its abandonment in the northern industrial towns and to a reversion to out-relief. Many agricultural districts had their own way of circumventing the Act, though their alternatives rarely proved successful. James Caird, in ENGLISH AGRICULTURE, 1850-51 (1852) *reported unfavourably on practices in Oxfordshire.*

The rates also are moderate, but the amount of poor rate is not always a safe indication of the weight of that burden on the farmer. In many parishes the farmers by agreement divide the surplus labour of the parish among them, to prevent the rates being swelled by the expense of supporting the unemployed. In so far they are benefited by getting something for their money. But it may be doubted whether such an arrangement is compatible with that economical subdivision of labour which ought to prevail on a

52 *A Refuge for the Destitute. This print in 1840 shows workhouse conditions following the Act of 1834*

well regulated farm, or whether a greater loss is not sustained by the example of unwilling labourers operating on the regular strength of a farm, than all the benefit received from their assistance. One farmer of 500 acres told us that he gave employment to twenty-six men and seven boys, which were seven men more than he required to do the work of his farm. Another had so many hands thrown upon him by this arrangement that he resorted to spade husbandry as the most profitable mode in which he could employ them. The addition of seven men on a farm of 500 acres is equivalent to an increase of nearly

6s. an acre of rent, and that is a very heavy charge to be laid exclusively on the tenant. . . .

Poor Law Reform in the Twentieth Century

A Royal Commission on the Poor Laws was appointed in 1905, but a divergence of opinion among its members led to the issue of two separate reports in 1909. The Majority Report proposed that the poor law system should be put under the control of county and borough councils (which was eventually carried out in 1929), but the MINORITY REPORT, *inspired by Beatrice and Sidney Webb, went beyond this to recommend the abolition of the poor law altogether, and the transference of poor relief to specialist committees, in the terms set out below. Both reports recognised the need for greater public responsibility.*

94. That the services at present administered by the Destitution Authorities (other than those connected with vagrants or the able-bodied)—that is to say, the provision for:—

(i.) Children of school age;

(ii.) The sick and the permanently incapacitated, the infants under school age, and the aged needing institutional care;

(iii.) The mentally defective of all grades and all ages; and

(iv.) The aged to whom pensions are awarded—should be assumed, under the directions of the County and County Borough Councils, by:—

(i.) The Education Committee;

(ii.) The Health Committee;

(iii.) The Asylums Committee and

(iv.) The Pension Committee respectively.

The Local Government Act (1929) finally transferred responsibility for the poor from the parish to the local authority. The Act of 1930, which followed up this transfer, reflected the government's concern at the rising cost of poor relief, and in places bore strong resemblances to the Act of 1601.

15—(1) It shall be the duty of the council of every county and county borough—

a) to set to work all such persons, whether married or unmarried, as have no means to maintain themselves, and use no ordinary and daily trade of life to get their living by;

b) to provide such relief as may be necessary for the lame, impotent, old, blind and such other persons as are poor and not able to work;

c) to set to work or put out as apprentices all children whose parents are not, in the opinion of the council, able to keep and maintain their children; and

d) to do and execute all other things concerning the matters aforesaid as to the council may seem convenient.

[POOR LAW ACT, 1930]

The RELIEF REGULATION ORDER OF 1930, *issued by the Minister of Health, showed that some progress had been made in poor law thinking, and a greater sense of social responsibility was evident than had been suggested above.*

. . . The council shall formulate such arrangements as may in the circumstances of their area be practicable for setting to work male persons who are capable of work (hereinafter referred to as 'able-bodied men') to whom relief other than institutional relief is afforded and for training and instructing such men in some physical form of useful work and for their attendance at suitable classes in physical training or of an educational character, and shall in such arrangements make due provision for securing that the work, training and instruction shall be suitable to the age, physical capacity and intelligence of the several classes of able-bodied men to whom the arrangements are intended to apply.

EPILOGUE

Our first and most essential proposal, which we have ourselves begun to implement in issuing this Report, is that all those interested should now take stock of their assumptions and ideas on the subject, and endeavour to work out an approach adapted to present and future rather than to past conditions. After a period of intensive growth the social services are settling down into the life of the nation. They are at present popular, and each taken by itself runs fairly smoothly, but they are creations of compromise and of improvisation, and every year that passes carries away more of the conditions on which they were based. A dangerous divergence therefore arises between the social and economic background (which corresponds less and less closely to that which the older social services were framed to meet) and the outlook and methods of administration which naturally tend to become less flexible as the service settles down to its routine. As everyone can observe, conditions and terms of treatment which are thought reasonable or inevitable at one period may come to be regarded as inhuman or intolerable a few years later.

[*PEP (Political and Economic Planning)*, REPORT ON THE BRITISH SOCIAL SERVICES, 1937]

LIST OF SOURCES

CHAPTER ONE

Helen Stocks (ed) *Records of the Borough of Leicester* 1603-1688 (1923)
David Davies *The Case of the Labourer in Husbandry* (1795)
Benjamin Disraeli *Sybil* or *The Two Nations* (1879)
G. Unwin *Industrial Organisation in the Sixteenth and Seventeenth Centuries* (Oxford 1904)
(for quotation from the Feltmakers' Court Book)
Daniel Defoe *A Tour Thro' the Whole Island of Great Britain by a Gentleman* (1724)
Adam Smith *The Wealth of Nations* (1776)
William Cobbett *Rural Rides* (1830)
Sir James Caird *English Agriculture* 1850-51 (1852)
B. Seebohm Rowntree *Poverty—A Study of Town Life* (1901)
R. E. Enfield *Agricultural Crisis* 1920-23 (1924)
Walter Greenwood *Love on the Dole* (1933)
HMSO *Report of the Ministry of Labour*, 1934
George Orwell *The Road to Wigan Pier* (1937)
William Beveridge *Unemployment: A Problem of Industry* (1909)

CHAPTER TWO

George Fox *Journal* 1694-8
John Wesley *Journal of John Wesley* (Bristol 1769)

John Wesley	*A Plain Account of the People called Methodists* (1749)
Guida Swan (ed)	*The Journals of Two Poor Dissenters* (1970)
Benjamin Disraeli	*Sybil* or *The Two Nations* (1879)
W. T. Stead	*Mrs Booth of the Salvation Army* (1900)
Arthur Barton	*Two Lamps in Our Street* (1967)
Richard Carew	*The Survey of Cornwall* (1602)
Joseph Strutt	*Sports and Pastimes of the People of England* (1801)
Edward Chamberlayne	*Angliae Notitia* or *The Present State of England* (1669)
William Windham	*Speeches in Parliament,* vol I (1812)
Robert Owen	*Observations on the Effect of the Manufacturing System* (1815)
Sir George Head	*A Home Tour Through the Manufacturing Districts of England* 1835 (1836)
Henry Mayhew	*London Labour and the London Poor* (1867)
Karl Baedeker	*London and Its Environs* (Leipsic 1900)
B. Bosanquet (ed)	*Social Conditions in Provincial Towns* (1912)
J. B. Priestley	*The Good Companions* (1929)

CHAPTER THREE

John Bruce (ed)	*Calendar of State Papers Domestic Series* 1629-31 (1860)
	The Gentleman's Magazine (1740)
Paul Mantoux	*The Industrial Revolution in the Eighteenth Century* (1928)
	(for quotation from the Wedgwood and Bentley Papers)
	Annual Register—1811
Sir James Caird	*English Agriculture* 1850-51 (1852)
Mrs Paget Toynbee (ed)	*Letters of Horace Walpole* (1903)
William Lovett and	
John Collins	*Chartism: a New Organisation of the People* (1840)
Thomas Cooper	*The Life of Thomas Cooper Written by Himself* (1872)
	The Times, 8 June 1934
	Leicester Journal, 7 February 1817
Robert Owen	Rules of the Grand National Consolidated Trades Union (1834)
	Annual Register—1872
	Labour Party Annual Conference Report (1907)
Randolph Churchill	*Winston S. Churchill,* Companion Volume II, Part 2 (1969)
Stanley Baldwin	*Our Inheritance* (1928)
Ellen Wilkinson	*The Town That Was Murdered* (1939)

CHAPTER FOUR

George Fox	*Advice and Warning to the Magistrates of London* (1657)
John Bellers	*Proposal for raising a College of Industry* (1696)
Robert Nelson	*An Address to Persons of Quality and Estate* (1715, reprinted Dublin 1752)

	The Gentleman's Magazine (1747)
Mrs Sarah Trimmer	*Reflections upon the Education of Children in Charity Schools* (1792)
K. and C. Fry	*Memoirs of the Life of Elizabeth Fry* (1847)
	Quarterly Review (1840)
	Illustrated London News, 12 April 1851
G. M. Young and W. D. Handcock	*English Historical Documents*, vol 12 (1956) (for the Report on Sanitary Conditions . . .)
D. K. & C. J. Guthrie	*Memoirs of Thomas Guthrie, DD* (1875)
Michael E. Rose	*The English Poor Law* 1780-1930 (Newton Abbot 1971) (for quotation from P. F. Ashcrott)
A. G. Gardiner	*The Life of George Cadbury* (1923)
	Annual Register—1935

CHAPTER FIVE

HMSO	*Acts of the Privy Council of England* (1964)
John Bruce (ed)	*Calendar of State Papers Domestic Series* 1629-31 (1860)
	Leicester Journal, 31 January 1817
Bland, Brown and Tawney	*English Economic History* (1914) (for quotation from *Parliamentary History*, vol 33 [1795-6])
	Reading Mercury, 11 May 1795
	Gin Act (1751)
	Coal Mines Regulation Act (1842)
Henry Mayhew	*London Labour and the London Poor* (1867)
	Truck Act (1831)
	Report of the Government Commission on Mines (1842)
	Ten Hours' Act (1847)
	Annual Register—1875
F. A. Iremonger	*William Temple, Archbishop of Canterbury* (1948)
	National Insurance Act (1911)
	Unemployment Assistance Act (1934)

CHAPTER SIX

	An Act for the Relief of the Poore (1601)
John Bruce (ed)	*Calendar of State Papers Domestic Series* 1629-31 (1860)
	Calendar of State Papers Domestic Series 1631-33 (1862)
	An Act . . . For the relief, and imployment of the Poor . . (1649)
Daniel Defoe	*Giving Alms No Charity* (1704)

W. Hutton	*An History of Birmingham* (1783)
George Crabbe	'The Village' (1783)
Thomas Malthus	*An Essay on the Principle of Population* (1798)
Joseph Lowe	*The Present State of England* (1822)
	Report from the Commission on the Poor Laws (1834)
Sir James Caird	*English Agriculture* 1850-51 (1852)
	Minority Report of the Royal Commission on the Poor Laws (1909)
	Poor Law Act (1930)
	Relief Regulation Order (1930)

EPILOGUE

Political and
Economic Planning

Report on the British Social Services (1937)

ACKNOWLEDGEMENTS OF ILLUSTRATIONS

The Mansell Collection, 1, 3, 5, 17, 18, 22 and 45
National Portrait Gallery, 4, 26, 30 and 35
British Museum, 8, 16, 20 and 21
Radio Times Hulton Picture Library, 10, 11, 23, 25,
  27, 28, 29, 31, 32, 33, 34, 37, 39, 41, 42, 43, 46, 50,
  51 and 52
Charles Hadfield, 44